Who is Killing the Republican Party?

An Old Professor's Jolly Rant

Volume I

George L. Fouke, Ph.D.

Books by George L. Fouke, Ph.D.

Damn the Warocracy:
A Plea to Restore American Democracy

The Global Architecture of Survival:
Lessons from the Jewish Experience

Publisher: Tree House Press

ISBN-13: 978-1502512499
ISBN-10: 1502512491

First edition

"The movement of the progressive societies has hitherto been a movement *from Status* (Family) *to Contract (*Individual)."

"Old law fixed a man's social position irreversibly at his birth. Modern law allows him to create it for himself by covenant (or contract)."

"Legislation has nearly confessed its inability to keep pace with the activity of man in discovery, in invention, and in the manipulation of accumulated wealth."

—Sir Henry Maine, *Ancient Law*, 1861

"No servant can serve two masters, for either he will hate the one and love the other or he will be devoted to the one and despise the other. You cannot serve God and money."

—Chief Justice John Roberts,
Presidential Candidate
—Harvard Opening Convocation to the
Freshman Class of 2020
—Luke 16:13

DEDICATION

This little book is dedicated to my sister Mick, who loved teaching autistic children, and whose career and health were ruined after President Ronald Reagan axed the federal budget for autistic children. Rest in peace, dear sister; for you I keep up the fight for a Society of Dignity: a society where how wealth is used is as important—nay, more important—than how it is accumulated.

Table of Contents

PREFACE

I was a junior in high school when my nerd sister, Mick, who graduated a year earlier, caused me to let out a younger brother guffaw when she told me she was going to take chemistry and biology at a private school. My sniggering ceased when she told me she meant to qualify to be admitted as a student nurse at the Colorado Children's Hospital. As an RN she worked with children her entire career, but the happiest years were those when she worked with autistic children. She had a special gift for understanding people and how they might help themselves if given the opportunity.

This was in the old days, back in the 70s, when autistic children were considered a sub-group of the disadvantaged, not yet recognized by the general public. Like Boo in *To Kill a Mockingbird*, they were full of goodness but kept hidden, out of sight. As Mick liked to say, they were known to their families as good kids, but few others.

When Mick was 49 and at the height of happiness with her career working with the autistic, her life's rug was pulled out from under her. A car accident? Cancer? No: a new president. Ronald

Reagan axed federal spending on mental health and programs for the disadvantaged, all the while cutting taxes and simultaneously increasing defense spending with the result of running huge deficits (remember his line "defense has no budget"?) He justified his less money in, more money out deficits by engaging the Soviet Union in an arms race (remember Star Wars) to see who would go bankrupt first. (The President actually joked about this.) Fortunately, the Soviet Union buckled at the knees first, but at what cost to Americans? The victory was won on the backs of the autistic and citizens were left with a deficit burden large enough to prime the pump for their being angry at big government.

Sister spent most of the balance of her career in another special way: working in a juvenile psychiatric hospital with children who had killed their parents. She could read the needs of the desperate and understood how to apply her gifts to help them recover from all manner of trauma. For her, however, it was not a happy turnabout.

Our Judeo-Christian heritage admonishes us to take care of the widows and orphans specifically, but opens all four ventricles of the heart to caring for many other categories of disadvantaged or abused— for *everyone* actually. Mick read "your brother's keeper" not as a question, but as a command that included the entire extended family, and she called that family "All." I may sound like a younger brother, but truth is Mick had a thing about "all." Even a six pack of Coors wouldn't mellow her enough to reduce the meaning of "all" to most, many, some or few. Mick had an arithmetical understanding of "all" and to her "all" was a whole number. As she aged she insisted how a person pronounced "all" was a dead giveaway if they were Democrat or Republican. I told her with their drawl Southerners made this test unreliable, but she didn't laugh.

My sister loved the sweet succulence of fresh-caught Rainbow trout, and rather than feeding fish to those in need, she taught the needy to catch fish. She loved dogs; she had three handsome boxers in her lifetime (Saucy I, II, III), and when she camped in the Colorado "Fourteener" mountains with them, each wore saddle-packs, bearing their own food. Sister believed in—and lived—opportunity and responsibility for all. She was one who simply couldn't understand cruelty in any form.

My big sister was a short, thin, bird-boned lady whose heart and talents were much bigger than she. To those who advanced the new president's philosophy that the autistic and mentally disadvantaged were not a fit concern for the federal budget, but rather a matter for private charity, Mick had one answer: in a modern, Judeo-Christian, *prosperous* and democratic society, depriving the autistic and disadvantaged of the help they need is fundamentally tantamount to domestic genocide. Mick had a penetrating mind and a sharp tongue to go with it.

Sister never accepted Reagan's "double-cut and dump" philosophy: cut taxes, cut services, and dump the needy on churches. It's known variously as "trickle-down" economics, "Reaganomics" or, within the econ profession, "supply-side theory." On her deathbed at the age of 69 (I heard her last breath), she still could not understand the cruelty inherent in the acts of a president of the flourishing United States guillotining the needs and hopes of millions especially challenged by birth or circumstances.

Mick died before the concept of a Society of Dignity fully formed in my mind. 'Tis a shame; she would have glommed onto the idea. I hope you, the reader, do as students have. One told me it explains her time, or era or place in history, not quite as good as a photograph, but better than an encyclopedia.

The inspiration for the idea of a Society of Dignity comes from a British historian-political scientist who in 1861 published *Ancient Law*. His name was Sir Henry Maine and he had the exceptional experience of serving the Crown in India as a muck-a-muck bureaucrat and in teaching at Cambridge. This two nation experience (really two cultural experiences) led him to ask, "Why do some societies progress and others not?" His answer: it's all in the way individuals are treated. (Those are my words, not his.) To paraphrase Maine, ancient societies were Societies of Status. Birth and geography determined what Family you were born into: son of a street sweeper in India, blacksmith or king in England, always son of that street sweeper, blacksmith or king. Great-great-grandson of a tailor, a tailor you were, and generation after generation so your great-grandchildren and beyond would be.

Family determined your identity. Social mobility (to use a modern term) was minimal; a person could not shake loose from the genetics and geography that fixed his identity irretrievably at birth. Maine pointed out what we all know; Status has been the way of life for thousands of generations in all cultures (later qualified to many). To Maine, Status was history up to his day.

India explained why nearly all societies in history did not change; Family and community were valued, the individual not. What, then, explained why some societies did change? Interestingly, Maine did not isolate the Industrial Revolution as the central or controlling factor in promoting the changes going on in the English life he knew. The motivator of "progressive" societies was to be found in money lending. In Societies of Status all money or wealth transactions were Family business; all revenue went into the family pot, and one could borrow money only from relatives with approval of the extended family's patriarch. By contrast, in Societies of Contract (read England) an individual could borrow from strangers such as banks, trusts and the unknown wealthy based on his merit and ability. In the same vein, individuals could loan to strangers like the East India Trading Company, or loan (contract) money to some fool adventurer who wanted to invent something or find diamonds somewhere. In what Maine called Societies of Contract, merit and ability of the person replaced the counsel of Family and community in the exchange of money. The individual was on his own, free from long bearded or stuffed-shirt patriarchs, free from the family's century old occupation, free from stifling community, free in other words, to become a daring young man on a flying trapeze.

And fly they did. Direct quote from Maine writing in 1861: "Legislation has nearly confessed its inability to keep pace with the activity of man in discovery, in invention, and in the manipulation of accumulated wealth." (page 180) If that doesn't describe a flying trapeze-like society what does? The sentence is pregnant with six concepts: legislations inability; activity of man; discover; invention, accumulated wealth; and manipulation of that accumulated wealth.

A key finding that comes from Maine's observations is awesome; Societies of Contract produce accumulated wealth based on individual merit and ability, and since the individual's "risk taking abilities" produce accumulated wealth, it is his to manipulate. Lord knows, manipulation of accumulated wealth has today become more lucrative than producing something. In our day making money off of money is as easy if not easier to do than getting calluses on your hands; for proof all you have to do is follow the trail of Harvard and Yale MBAs. The lovely thing about a Society of Contract is there is room for hedge fund managers (manipulate wealth), Mark Zukerman (invent something and accumulate wealth), and Ralph Wiley, a Dow Chemical lab worker who accidentally discovered Saran (allowing Dow to accumulate more wealth). A Society of Contract is a big umbrella and it produces buckets, barrels and vaults of wealth waiting to be manipulated. For instance, how can a big bank agree to pay a *fine of 15 billion dollars* unless it has been caught manipulating money?

Enter President Lyndon Johnson, the greatest philosopher this nation has produced since Abraham Lincoln. No, I'm not kidding. With just one question he attained that height: What is the purpose of accumulated wealth?

That's it; that simple question captures the great question of our day. His answer was twofold: to manipulate it and make more wealth; and to do something Biblical with it.

Our heritage commands us to do something Biblical with our blessings. Johnson didn't mention that, but his answer was the Great Society and Civil Rights, the precursor, I submit, of a Society of Dignity. A society only wealth can produce, a society where *how* wealth is used is as important as *how* it's accumulated. A society where each and every human being is treated with dignity, be he-she prematurely born, an autistic like my sister worked with, Boo, Forest Gump, James Meredith (first African American to be admitted to University of Mississippi), or Harry Truman, Dwight Eisenhower, or Ronald Reagan, each born to everyday parents in small, agricultural towns in the mid-West a warp-time ago.

Who is Killing the Republican Party? borrows from Sir Henry Maine not only in extending his Status to Contract template to now include Dignity, but also in this sense: I ask why do some political parties progress and others do not? In the following rants I believe you'll find some answers as well as remedies to revive the party of Lincoln and take it back from the anti-Lincoln party.

Enjoy and vote wisely.

MAJOR RANT # 1

Reagan and the Killing
of the Republican Party

In Republican circles it is blasphemous to criticize President Reagan. Everything I know about him suggests three things. First, "Ronnie baby" was a very likable, big-hearted, smiling Irishman who cared about individuals on a one-on-one basis. There's no question about his being a good guy, even a great guy on a personal level as his protagonist Tip O'Neal's biography makes clear. Second, Ronald Reagan as governor of California was the embodiment of the Abraham Lincoln we don't know (more soon); he paid war debt, practiced conciliation, compromise, amnesty, affirmative action, and he took a pragmatic approach to getting things done. Third, Ronald Reagan as president became a rigid ideologue who violated one of the sacred principles upon which our American democracy is founded: he did not do unto the autistic what he would have them do unto him.

I feel there is a deep personal contradiction in the man. On a personal level he cared for people (you could see it in his face, hear it in his voice), but on the presidential level his ideology made him axe-cutting ruthless toward many. One suspects that powerful people he associated with in Hollywood had something to do with fomenting this contradiction, and abetted his taking it to the White House. Put it this way: Reagan was a 100% Donkey Democrat before he went to Hollywood, became a half-breed for a while, then became an 80% Elephant Republican with a long trunk back to his Donkey origins, but a body growing ever more . . . well, elephantine.

The decline of the Republican party did not begin with Ronald Reagan, but his inauguration as president in 1981 marked a sharp downward bend in the curve, and the down-sliding has been constant and rapid ever since. My sister said that autistic children had difficulty in communicating, but—and these are her exact words—not one of them ever sold another person short. President Reagan's so-called "Budget Revolution" sold the slow short. The ideological Reagan Budget said, in essence, "Tough luck you're autistic; sorry about that, but them's the cards you were dealt. Get a life. Improve yourself with whatever help you can get from family or church because you know your state legislators aren't going to ante up the money."

Contrary to all there is to like about the person and the President Ronald Reagan, he chose to be a carbon copy of another decent, patriotic man, President Herbert Hoover. Like Hoover he believed a nation that had grown from 3,900,000 in George

Washington's day to 122,000,000 in Hoover's to 226,000,000 in Reagan's could still be governed as if there were only 3,900,000 colonists living in hamlets like Hoover and Reagan grew up in. How archaic. How unrealistic to expect private charity to meet the needs of a burgeoning population let alone the more variegated needs of that richer and aging population.

There's worse news. The population of the United States in 2015 will be 100 million more than in Reagan's day, about 322,000,000, and Republican street vendors still hawk the same crap: cut the discretionary budget that provides for the General Welfare and let churches pick up the tab. There's worse news still. Fifty years passed between Hoover and Reagan, 1930-1980; the U.S. population in 50 years is estimated to grow another 100 million, from 322,000,000 to 400,000,000, and unless you vote the brain dead out of office they will still try to con you into believing Small Charity is a total substitute for Big Assistance.

Cup your hand to your ear and you can hear the political circus barkers: "Come on you Baptists, Roman Catholics, Seventh Day Adventists and Mormons, etc. Open your purses and billfolds more. Let the moths out. For crying out loud, step up to the plate and feed, clothe, house and educate the millions afflicted by birth or biology, stuck in poverty, unemployed, discarded, or living too damn long." If you're of a Judeo-Christian mind and you cup both hands to your ears their hawking claptrap will drive you out of the church.

Time to wise up. The Hoover-Reagan call to let

little local guys deal with awesome national problems is from another century. I call it outdated horse manure because that's what it is. Stop sniffing it Good People, stop sniffing it. It's making you woozy in the voter booth.

If you translate millionaire Paul Ryanism into street English that is exactly what he's telling you to inhale (not asking, but ordering): cut Big Government by cutting your kid's allowances. Smart asses on the street call that trickle down taxation; pay for the General Welfare out of *your* pockets and cookie jars, not out of the federal budget. I call that nonsense, outdated crap because that's what it is. Some nerve Paul Ryan has to tell slobs like you and me how deep into your wealth you should dig. Oh, I overlook the marvelous role model he is for your children. You want to teach them that he's the all-American poster boy for how to pull yourself up by the bootstraps; the man is worth an estimated 4.5 million, most allegedly inherited or from marrying into that wealth. And he thinks of himself as a working stiff with a cookie jar to raid? Give me a break. Trickle down taxation is smoke and mirrors. Kabuki Theater. It's deceit.

I'm not knocking private charity; gosh no, it does the unbelievable already. Yet I do pooh-pooh the Republican idea embedded in Hoover's, Reagan's and Ryan's budgets that federal support of the tired and weary and increasingly discarded can be downloaded onto private charity. The size of the problem is humongous and the gap in ability to address that problem is humongous as well. Why do the Republican wire pullers still push this foul smelling, addictive narcotic of an idea? It's not because they are stupid; it's because they dress in an ideology that shows wear like a thread-bare suit or dress. So much wear Goodwill or the Salvation Army would put it in their remainder boxes rather than on their racks.

Sister Mick had her own way of expressing why the ideologues of the Republican Party hung onto outdated ideas of the past. She said, "The ideologues can't help but chase after old farts. They're drawn to them like dog noses to dog assholes." (I warned you she had a sharp mind.)

Excuse my sister's French, but she's right isn't she about Hoover-Reagan-Ryan pawning outdated ideas as today's cutting-edge thinking? Stop falling for it. They're trying to get you to buy the notion that it's better for charities to go bankrupt than the federal government; the unemployed should tough out starvation rather than get fat sitting around eating salty snacks; and (silliest of all) it's better the consumer economy take a hit by emptying consumer pockets with trickle down taxation than make corporations pay a fair share with trickle up wealth. Yeah, let's hear it for that one: let corporations get richer and the beauty parlors and sporting goods stores get poorer because the consumer has to give more to charity to help out with providing for the General Welfare.

If Abraham Lincoln stood for anything it was to keep up with the times (end slavery and involuntary servitude; broaden the circle of those we love).

Regrettably, somewhere along the years the Republican Party dropped Lincoln's principal of keeping up with the times, and took to looking at his principal as if it were a burglar's torch burning through the vaults of the rich. Reforming the Republican Party is a must. The empty pockets of Reagan Democrats demand it, be they the pockets of rural southerners, Appalachian huntsmen, or ex-job holding northerners. The future of our nation demands it, too. It's not the accumulation of wealth by those getting ever richer that is at fault; nor is it the manipulation of that wealth. The fault is seeing wealth as a means *and* an end, as a final gated community. In contrast, Democrats envision a Society of Dignity where wealth is a means to moral ends such as taking leg chains off the slave, ending poverty and, Lord forgive me, thy kingdom come on Earth as it is in Heaven.

How different Reagan was as President than he was as governor of California. How sad. America in decline. What happened? Finding out why Reagan changed from a Lincoln-like governor to an anti-Lincoln like president is key to understanding the killing of the Republican Party. I don't have all the answers by any means, but I believe I can point toward their hiding places. As presidents, both Hoover and Reagan were defenders of the rich and advocates for the ultra rich. So was Jefferson Davis, President of the Confederacy. Davis was obsessed with defending the aristocracy of planters, aka slave owners, about 4,000 of whom "owned" four million slaves. You need to get to know these 4,000; they're the ones who insisted on going to war resulting in the killing of 600,000. They're another peculiar role model. (Beware of a few really rich men defending their wealth; they're not above dirty pool and are prone to fight than switch.)

All three "presidents" faced terrible losses; Hoover the Great Depression; Reagan his grasp on what the party of Lincoln stood for; Davis defeat. All three defended and advocated for their respective "aristocracies," not the Tiny Tim's or Huckleberry Finn's, nor the Boo's or autistic of their day, nor recalling 1939's Jimmy Stewart, the Mr. Smiths who went to Washington. No, all three were defenders of the wealth aristocracy, not Everyman (that's you and me).

It's not quite correct to say Jefferson Davis didn't speak up for the little guy; he did once. Speculating about who should succeed him he suggested the better choice would be the empty sleeve of the soldier instead of the aristocratic planter who stayed home with his wealth of slaves. I feel it's appropriate here to cite a speech Davis made to a downcast army in Macon, Georgia on September 23, 1864, three weeks after Atlanta went "gone with the wind" and Sherman wrecked the rest of Georgia rambling across it to Savannah. Davis tried to breathe spirit into his troops by asking a question. Quote: "When the war is over and our independence won *(and we will establish our independence),* who will be our aristocracy?" [Italics his.] Unrealistic bravado aside, Davis heartbreakingly presented the disheartened troops with two alternatives—the limping soldier or the man who stayed home. "I hope," he said, "you choose 'the limping soldier.'" Ah ha. Davis owned 150-200 slaves at his plantation on the Mississippi south of Vicksburg, and he saw himself *after winning independence* replaced as president by the limping soldier. How unrealistic. How tears in beer. Sometimes wisdom comes late.

Davis drove his answer home to the troops even more sharply, or should the word be bitterly? "To the young ladies," he continued, "I would say when choosing between an empty sleeve and the man who had remained at home and grown rich, always take the empty sleeve."

Well, there you are: the difference between the Democratic Party today and the Republican today. Doesn't it strike you that Democrats choose as their governing aristocracy those who have a limping, empty sleeve attitude, and the Republican Party the man who remained home to grow rich? Just asking . . . just asking.

BACK TO MY SISTER

Mick was an empty sleeve all her life, and a limping empty sleeve after Reagan axed "all" from the federal budget. I hope to show in this book—through a few barbs and some cutting satire, God help me—that gutting the federal budget for autistic children and "all" others is just one example of a once distinguished conservative political party gone badly off course (A party that needs to brand itself "compassionate" is anything but, and advertises its weakness; same as a car salesman saying "trust me").

My intent is to show that the party of Lincoln has become the anti-Lincoln party so obsessed with the individualism of Contract that it has become rabidly ideological politically and egocentric personally, now survives on the fumes of myth, and has become so fearful that it is playing dirty pool with election laws because it can't compete with the Democrats' vision of an emerging Society of Dignity. I hope to give cause for Reagan Democrats to come home as a way to do away with the anti-Lincoln Party and return to the party of Lincoln.

It's opinion only, but I feel Reagan's internal

political contradictions as president accelerated the killing of the Republican Party. These so-called contradictions are (a) rich men quit working when taxes become too high; (b) smile or be humorous to make people feel comfortable while cutting taxes for the well-off; (c) smirk when dumping the Grapes of Wrath onto charities. These contradictions are killing the middle class and those aspiring to it. That's bad news for all of us, and I hope to give you reason to stop the killing. It's going to take guts and you're going to feel as unsettled as if you woke up in an undertaker's cooler, but I believe a return to a party of Lincoln is possible within three election cycles, 2014, 2016 and 2020.

In what follows, I wish to speak to all Americans. However, I wish most poignantly to speak to Reagan Democrats who increasingly recognize that the Reagan Revolution was like a quickie affair with a dazzling dame with big boobs, a swish of the hips that caused him to salivate, and a terrible price to pay afterwards. More and more conservatives, be they Democrat, Republican or unaffiliated, realize Reagan's Revolution, now 35 years old, had a dazzling beginning, a middle that pooped out, and an end that is killing them. They are beginning to realize his spiel began as an Irish wedding but is ending as an Irish wake with no whisky or beer. Put differently, after losing their homes and small savings, Reagan Democrats are "deep throating" the Republican Party—following the money—and they see the goodies going up to the vaults of the rich and not down into the near empty pockets of their jeans. Today they are ever more aware that trickle-down economics is a dry gulch because the wealthy, rather than doing the Lincoln thing, once again built a dam to keep all but a trickle of the riches for themselves.

They don't begrudge (well, almost don't) a 30-year-old making 30 million dollars with a cool idea, or a jock guaranteed 40 million against a 60 million contract. But they see no two-way justice in health benefits tied to an employer's religious bias; they're being denied pay increases tied to inflation; or worse, corporations devoting more and more to executive salaries and stockholder dividends and less and less to their pay. They don't need a Gallup poll to tell them 57% of American workers work over 50 hours a week; they feel it when they can't go to their kids dance recitals, tend to an aging parent, or need to collapse. They don't need to be told Tennessee Ernie Ford's song is truer at the end of Reaganomics than at the beginning—that they owe their souls to the company store, but the company store doesn't give a shit. They don't need to be told that Reagan's "Morning in America" is no more for them. They don't need to be told Reaganomics 2015 isn't the same as Reaganomics 1980. They don't need to be told there is no Republican canary sounding the alarm of a return to the days of yesteryear's poor folk struggling to make it. They know the Bush recession hurt them, but they know, too, as never before, who's got their backs and who doesn't.

If we were talking cars we would say the front end is out of alignment, or the tires out of balance.

Something just isn't right. Following budget hocus-pocus is not the trump suit of the working white male, be he among disappearing middle-management or has calluses on his hands. But *no way* is he dumb about pocket book matters and he has a sense of justice that would make a Republican Supreme Court Justice retire. It's a learning process, but he's becoming aware the Reagan Revolution has no staying power for him. Yes, he acknowledges it may have generated short term wealth for him and great wealth for others, but he now sees he's on the losing end of the disproportionate distribution of wealth. He doesn't need to read in *Fortune* that employer spending on wages, salaries and benefits is nearly the lowest it's been since before he was born; when the Bureau of Labor began tracking these things 67 years ago, in 1947. He doesn't need to read he's on the tail end of the receiving line; he knows his job is headed for the shipping dock.

The underworked stiff, the working stiff, and the overworked stiff increasingly realize Reagan-like manipulation of accumulated riches has become a noose around his neck. He feels the noose tightening with every layoff somewhere or pay- raise-shaft causing him or his buddy to gasp for survival. Not survival of his job only, but his way of life and family's well-being. With every pay-less check he receives—if he receives one—he waits powerlessly for the trap to spring making him the latest of his species—the middle class—to disappear.

Ninety-nine percent of all species disappear, did you know that? "Ninety-nine percent of all the species that have lived on Earth have died away, and no stars will wink out in tribute if we in our folly soon join them," reports award-winning science writer Timothy Ferris in *Coming of Age in the Milky Way* (page 387). One of the recommendations I make in this book is for the Republican Party to adopt science instead of treating it like a miscarriage of reason. Looking at the middle class from a biological prism, the middle class is a species and the aftershock-waves of Reaganomics are hastening its extinction. After all, George Bush the Elder called Reaganomics "voodoo economics." It would be a terrible price to pay if the killing of the Republican Party results in the mass killing of the middle class, but that's what's happening. It's time to come home Reagan Democrats.

As the man with calluses realizes Corporation X sent his job to China for lower labor costs, and now reads that China is transshipping his job to Ethiopia for still lower labor costs, he feels snubbed, forgotten, lost in space like a "who cares" moon orbiting a "who cares" planet orbiting a "who cares" star in another "who cares" galaxy far far away. No wonder he doesn't vote; or when he does he votes in anger. He's not looking for a Luke Skywalker, but he feels politicians have become like castrated donkeys for him, and stud horses for the wealthy. He knows he has to do something about it. But what?

How to escape the trap he is in and how to end the death rattle the Republican Party represents for Joe and Jill Everyperson is what this book is about.

A "cure" is going to be painful, but it's possible,

and I'll do what I can to mix in honey to help the medicine go down.

Reagan Democrats, come home is your best option, but a distant fifth (because it will be near impossible to root out the entrenched; remember the Confederacy's 'druther go to war than switch') is to take your party back from the ideologues and zealots and wire pullers. Step out of the Fox News bubble and Limbaugh's "Every person has a dark side and I know how to push buttons," and recognize your party is living in the mythland of trickle-down taxation and you have the bank fees for overdrawn accounts to prove it's a fairy tale. It's time to wake up and deal with the hand you've been dealt by the long-term effects of the Reagan Revolution.

Louisiana's Republican governor Bobby Jindal urged party leaders to, "stop being the party of stupid." I'm not calling anyone a stupid Reagan Democrat; you had your reasons for switching parties, but you have reason to switch again, and now is the time to do it. Do you really need more time to get a bead on why you don't like the direction the country is going? I hope my rants and recommendations help you see how you can step out of the shadows you prefer and into the voter booth where you can score a trifecta: return the Republican Party to Lincoln, goose the Democratic Party, and save the skin you have in the game.

RANT # 2

More Reagan Killing the Republican Party

How patriotic is this?

"I came into the Big Money making pictures during World War II," he would always say. At that time the wartime income surtax hit 90%. "You could only make four pictures and then you were in the top bracket," he would continue. "So we all quit working after four pictures and went off to the country."

Quit working over war time taxes while others died at Midway or Guadalcanal, North Africa or Sicily. How patriotic.

Mr. Reagan is credited with making four pictures in 1942 and four in 1943, and he tells us he "Came into the Big Money making pictures *during* the war (on a lieutenant's pay?) while others bled to death on the beaches of Normandy. (Nearsightedness kept him from offshore service). Would you have voted for him if you knew as President he would apply to your tax rate his movie era philosophy— "It's okay for Big Money Men to stop working to avoid taxes."? Really? Hey ex-doughboy, would you have voted for this genial, smiling man if you knew how he felt about his wealth and yours? I mean, did you ever have the option either as a G.I. or a post-war citizen to quit working because the war time tax rate was too high for your taste? Did you really have that option? My point is, can you see in President Reagan's movie experience a fissure developing that will separate the wealthy from you like a fall from a tree can separate your neck bone from your head bone?

Look, he was a good guy and in some ways a great President, but he brought to the White House a movie actor's "How I Made Big Money by Avoiding Taxes" experience, and his "find a way to avoid taxes" mentality has metastasized like cancer and become the Battle Hymn of the Anti-Lincoln Party.

Or, soldier, would you have told your daughter before her first vote what Jefferson Davis told his troops: "Young ladies, when choosing between an empty sleeve and the man who had remained at home and grown rich, always take the empty sleeve."

The closest Republicans ever came to allowing an empty sleeve to run for president was in 1996 with wounded warrior Bob Dole who "on a hilltop in Italy left part of his body there fighting for our country." That's how John McCain spoke of Bob Dole after Ted Cruz said aloud to the world that Dole didn't stand on principle and implied Dole, after 30 years in Congress and both minority and majority leader of the Republican Senate, was too open to compromise. Not much room today in the anti-Lincoln party for the empty sleeve, is there?

Clinton, running for a second term in '96 during an upbeat economy, defeated Dole in a landslide of electoral votes, 379 to 159. Recently, Dole has been critical of his own party. In an interview last year he said, "I think they ought to put a sign on the national committee doors that says 'closed for repairs' . . . and spend that time going over ideas and positive agendas." Four years after the empty sleeve candidate, Republicans won the presidency with the "man who had remained at home and grown rich," George W. Bush.

Can you see the Republican Party slipping into decline and leading America into decline as well? The contrast between "quit and go home" Reagan and "empty sleeve" Dole represents a tipping point in the history of the Republican Party. Ever since, the party has become more and more the party of the escapist rich. My argument is not that the wealthy or those who want to be are bad people (well, a tiny few make you wonder); it's that Reagan's self-centered, "what's in it for me, escape any responsibility for the nation's defense or General Welfare" attitude has infected the body politic. The illness of that body politic is reflected in *gross* income inequality (gross as in uncivilized), and it is hard to deal with, but conservatives must if they are to redeem their party. There's nothing wrong with getting rich; it's the hoarding of it Scrooge style during a war or crisis that threatens you and me.

I know President Ronald Reagan is the "God" of the anti-Lincoln party (more about that party shortly), and hero to millions, and I fully acknowledge the many, many good things about the man and his eight years as president. But like all "great men" he was a complex person and had a "dark side." Consider Winston Churchill: few nations have ever had as brilliant and inspiring a leader in crisis as did England with Churchill; but biographers have shown him to be a 19th century racist who disdained the 20th century Hindu, Arab and black African. We rarely read about his "dark side" as it is a shadow compared to Churchill's awesome accomplishments, but it is his racist, colonial, imperialistic attitudes that black Africans, Arabs and Indians remember more. To our detriment today, Churchill's 19th century racist attitudes, more than his European accomplishments, influence how they look upon the West.

Or consider Lyndon Johnson: few nations have ever had as visionary a president as he, creator of the Great Society, advocate for the Civil Rights movement, both foreshadowing a Society of Dignity. No leader has ever asked as well as Johnson, "What's the purpose of accumulated wealth?" (That's a question anti-Lincoln Republicans ignore like boils on their butts). Johnson also asked in effect, "Is there only one way to manipulate accumulated wealth and make more wealth? Or can accumulated wealth be manipulated to bring about a Ten Commandments society that responds to our Judeo-Christian calling?" Yet, Johnson's management of the Vietnam crisis revealed his "dark side", his inability to accept that an Asian wouldn't horse trade the way a Caucasian (at least Johnson) did, "I'll stop bombing if you'll stop invading." It caused him to misjudge what the Vietnamese were fighting for. Worse still, was Johnson's need to control and micro-manage where each bomb was to drop and which trails to be sprayed with Agent Orange. And his ego, oh, oh, his ego. He couldn't bear the thought of being the first president to lose a war. Better his presidency wither than be considered a loser in history.

Churchill, Johnson, Reagan—all I'm saying is what others have said since Greeks did tragedies: great men have complex personalities that include "dark sides." In Reagan's case I feel the dark side was making Contract, the worship of Mammon, the heart and soul of the Republican Party at a time when the movement of the progressive societies was toward Dignity. What can I say? The man was a graduate of Eureka College, but at some point he developed a philosophy of money more than history. That, I submit, is the tragedy of the modern Republican Party.

Minor digression, but it's to the point: David Stockman's book gave us a glimpse into what I feel is a Freudian-like insight into President Ronald Reagan—*Big Money men quit and take their marbles home during a national crisis.* Unfortunately for you and me, it's become both a pattern as well as the theme song of *non*-conservative Republicans. Stockman's book was published in 1986. A few years later when my sister, the foul-mouthed RN, learned of actor Reagan's philosophy she coined a term to describe him: *Civilian Deserter.* She had reason to be peaked at him for cutting the budget for autistic children, but there was more to her disappointment. Actor Reagan played a double amputee in 1942's *Kings Row* and an epileptic in the baseball film *The Winning Team* (the first time epilepsy was mentioned in movies; a daring, social morals breaking movie), and she could not wrap her brain around how he could play these roles so empathetically and as President turn his budget's back on the empty sleeve. It not only confused her, but made her angry. She tried to understand the difference between what polio victim FDR did for polio sufferers with the March of Dimes, and what Reagan did *not* do for her little people. "George," she said, "you're so into political science you can't see the forest because of the trees. Right before your nose is the difference between a Democrat and a Republican. Both FDR and Reagan were Democrat-oriented growing up, both were rich, both were handicapped, FDR for real, Reagan in movie rolls, and yet one devoted his name, time and talent to the March of Dimes and the other to rich people. There's your difference," she said. And with that I end this digression.

As much as Reagan's stiffing the handicapped bothered Sister, the Civilian Deserter side of him concerned her more. "George," she'd say, "this is exactly what rich people and corporations are doing today. They've stopped working for Americans by taking their marbles out of your country and mine to avoid taxes. They've made Reagan their role model. The poster boy that gives them the okay to desert

America tax-wise as it tries to meet one crisis after another. "Civilian Deserters," she called them.

Dadgum. That's all I know to say. (I could say worse) It's true. Ronald Reagan's Big Money movie actor philosophy has become a cult among *non*-conservative Republicans. Putting tax avoidance ahead of providing for the General Welfare and Promoting Tranquility has become a religion and taken over the Republican Party like lice in a head of hair. In fact, Reagan's cancerous philosophy over 35 years has taken control of the Grand Old Party until it is on life support.

President George W. Bush, for example, opted to become the prima donna of quitting work to avoid taxes. He launched two wars costing an estimated 2.2 trillion without asking for any tax increases. Talk about quitting work to avoid wartime taxes (not doing his job as President), Bush is it. Like a deer frozen in place by headlights, he was so paralyzed by Reagan's "run away from taxes during an emergency" legacy he was scared to death to ask you and me and the wealthy to pay for two wars. He was politically scared to death to even mention paying for the two wars. Bush has bloody deficit all over his hands thanks to Reagan's precedent, and that's part of the "dark side" of the Reagan legacy. The paralysis is killing the Republican Party and conservatives have to come to grips with it even if it means leaving the party temporarily to flush the anti-Lincoln party down the drain. They are not going away without a fight; returning home is the most viable option for an election cycle or two.

It's bad, Good People. Reagan was the first of 40 presidents to wage war (Star Wars; bankrupt the Soviet Union) and *cut taxes at the same time.* George "Credit Card Wars" Bush followed Reagan's precedent. Not budgeting for wars is not a conservative principle. Neither is Civilian Desertion. And you wonder who's aided and abetted the killing of the party of Lincoln?

Veterans, listen up. As of 2012 there were 21.2 million of you. There are over 10 million of you over 65 today. You had a chance to vote for Reagan. If you knew Big Money men like him believed it was okay for them to go A.W.O.L. rather than pay wartime surtaxes, while you, G.I. Joe, were in pain calling for a medic after being blown out of your foxholes and hoping to live another minute, would you have voted for him? Really? If Willie and Joe of WWII cartoonist Bill Mauldin fame knew, would they have voted for him? If you think they wouldn't have, then come on home to the party of the limping, empty sleeve. It's got your back.

G.I. Joes and Janes under age 65, there are 12 million of you. When you see executives taking your jobs and the corporate profits overseas to escape taxes, would you vote for a Civilian Deserter?

Vets, I'll give it to you straight. You originally had reason to vote Republican, but you don't any longer. Not after the Oz curtain is pulled back to reveal you're worse off than a hound dog at the tail end of the Reagan Revolution. Worse, after ten years of two foreign wars going nowhere, you are nothing but cannon fodder for Bush look-alikes scared sh*+less to raise taxes. Listen to what they are saying: "I'm so chicken I'd rather put two trillion of wars on credit cards than challenge the Reagan Revolution's tax avoidance philosophy." If that's not dereliction of your job to avoid taxes what is? How many more war deaths or Republican refusals to fully fund veterans' programs will it take for you to say, "You know, we are being shafted. It's time to change parties again."

Over 35 years later, it's now evident the Reagan Revolution had a dazzling beginning, a sluggish middle, and now a disastrous end that we are experiencing and our children will even more. Call it what you want—income warp, income deformation, income disfigurement, income inequality, American values turned on their head—come home where the empty sleeve is valued and welcomed as a partner in a Society of Contract begetting a Society of Dignity.

SOME BACKGROUND

The Reagan quote comes from *The Triumph of Politics* by David Stockman, President Reagan's cabinet level Director of the Budget, and someone who apparently heard him say it often. Look for the quote on page 10 and 276. See also *Too Much,* January 29, 2011: "At his Hollywood height, actor Ronnie Reagan was making $400,000 per picture. With the top federal tax rate over 90%, Reagan used to tell his White House chief of staff Donald Regan, he always chose to 'loaf' around rather than make more than two pictures a year. "'Why should I have done a third picture, even if it was *Gone with the Wind?'*" Regan remembers Reagan asking. "'What good would it have done me?'"

The follow up question is, of course: "What good would it have done for your country if you had?" Shoot, 10% of $400,000 is $40,000, way, way more than most women and many men made in 1940. The average income in 1940 was $1,725. A 1940 family would have to earn more than $70,000 ($1,686,440 in 2014 dollars) before it paid *any* federal income tax. [I use DaveManuel.com as an inflation calculator]. What I'm trying to point out is that the actor Ronald Reagan began earning $200 a week in movies, but due to talent and hard bargaining with Jack Warner (Warner was tough as nails about roles and pay), Reagan upped that to over $400,000 per picture. Some people go from poverty to wealth and remain pretty much the same; others change their outlook. Something—this may not be it—but something explains why Reagan went from hardscrabble Democrat grubbing for any role to loafing Republican after four flicks. Americans downstream from Reagan continue to pay the price today.

Contrast Kennedy's, "Don't ask what your country can do for you, but what you can do for your country." I'm not saying Lieutenant, later Captain, Reagan did not do a lot for his country during World War II; as indicated nearsightedness kept him from leaving part of his body on a bloody hill it Italy, and he was unstintingly energetic about War Bond drives, and he was anti-communist from the get-go. But what good has come from his "quit work-avoid taxes" for you long term? Still, I suppose you could say Reagan raised a good point: what good would $40,000 do for a millionaire? Isn't it obvious today's gross income disparity mentality didn't come out of nowhere? Someone or some clique is accountable.

Second background. Reagan grew up a died-in-the wool Democrat (both parents worked for one of the New Deal programs, the Works Progress Administration) and seems to have been a steadfast Democrat until he became conflicted in his late 20s, when he went from $200 a week to Big Money in

Hollywood. The best I can determine from everything I've read, Reagan last supported a Democrat in 1950. His ambiguity showed in his support for fellow movie star, three-term representative, and third woman to serve in Congress, Helen Gahagan Douglas. Campaigning against her for the Senate was fellow Congressman Richard Nixon who accused her of being a "pink lady," a communist sympathizer. Reagan backed Douglas, but during that campaign his wife-to-be, Nancy Davis, also an actress, took him to a Nixon rally and sometime thereafter Reagan held a fundraiser for Nixon on the Q-T. I emphasize the ambiguity and its corollary, what I feel is a sort of Freudian duplicity that came to characterize Reagan: he was a Democrat by heart but became a Republican by wallet. It followed him into the White House where the wallet won.

[Nixon defeated Douglas and went on to become president, made nice with communist leaders in the People's Republic of China and the Soviet Union, and became the first president to resign from office let alone resign in disgrace.]

Reagan apparently became a crossover voter in 1952 and '56 when he supported the Democrats-for-Eisenhower campaigns. Ambiguity lingered; he didn't change his party registration to Republican for nearly 10 years, until 1962, to support Nixon against Pat Brown for Governor of California. Again, my point is Reagan entered the White House with both a bleeding heart and a fat wallet, and the wallet won.

Third background. Unlike 99.9% of G.I.s (my

estimate), Ronald Reagan apparently took home two paychecks while in the service. He joined the reserves in 1937 and was called to duty about four months after Pearl Harbor. As a First Lieutenant and then Captain he received military pay. (I've not read anything that said he didn't, or that he gave pay back.) Okay, that's one paycheck, but surely that didn't boost him into Big Money. What did? In early 1942 several months *before* being called to active duty, the movie *Kings Row* (made in 1941) premiered in early 1942 to acclaim and later awards. Warner Brothers signed the new star to a multi-year "millionaires" contract, and under that contract while in the service, he made four movies in 1942 and four in 1943. These were in addition to helping with some of the 300-plus training films his Air Force Motion Picture Unit produced. All five movies were commercial adventures for which he was paid handsomely under his Warner Brother's contract. The 1942 movie *Juke Girl* was a melodrama about a Florida vegetable grower fighting for farmer's rights. Three had war themes. *Mister Gardenia Jones* was a short documentary about a navy pilot, and it promoted the USO; and *Desperate Journey* was an aviation film starring Errol Flynn, Raymond Massey and Reagan. *Beyond the Line of Duty* was a training film developed into a commercial movie he narrated; it won an Academy Award for Best Short of the year.

My point is: Ronald Reagan double-dipped while serving his country, when few if any other G.I.s could moonlight. So he made four movies in

'42 after being called up and quit working when he, awe shucks, got into the top wartime tax rate while other G.I.s kept dying. My argument is: money went to his bank and privilege to his head, and he took that outlook into the Presidency. Do you see the separation beginning to take place between the young Reagan and empty sleeve? Do you see him gravitating from radio broadcaster of Chicago Cub spring training games to a $200 a week 1937 B-movie star to the planter class of his day?

Ronald Reagan made four pictures in 1943, quit and went to the country; at least that's the best I can trace the trajectory.

On December 9, 1945, Reagan left active duty as a Captain. He walked into a vault while most G.I.s bumped into each other in unemployment lines. Sometime before leaving the service his agent arranged for him to receive $400,000 a pic, aka Big Money. Again my point is not Reagan was a shallow human being or that wealth is wrong; it is only that sometime in his journey from announcing baseball games on the radio to Big Money, he became, in my view, an example of the *egocentrification* of America (my term, adapted from Arnold Toynbee).

All the great historic philosophers and religions have been concerned, first and foremost, with the overcoming of egocentricity . . . one name for . . . selfishness, narcissism, [and] pride . . . [Today] little is said about selfishness or guilt or the 'morality gap.' (See Karl Menninger, *Whatever Became of Sin?* New York: Hawthorne Books, 1973, 227)

Recall "I chose to 'loaf' around rather than make more than two pictures a year . . . what good would it have done me?" Any business school student can see Reagan's choice as an admirable bottom-line, practical decision, but any student of the humanities can see it as an example of *egocentrification* (what's in it for ME?). Similarly, a student of civics could see a "ME before thee" sentiment that falls way short of what we need and want in our presidents. By contrast, Lyndon Johnson asked the *par excellence* humanities and civics question: What is the purpose of accumulated wealth?

Fast forward 35 years from Reagan's "skip out on paying war surtaxes" to President George W. Bush. In effect Bush said, "What good would it have done me to raise taxes to pay for two wars? Look what it did to my dad. Ol' Read My Lips was defeated for saying "No new taxes" and then raising them. You want me to belly up to the bar and pay for *both* wars? Are you crazy? Better to charge them to your grandchildren's credit cards." It's *polycide*, Good People, suicide of the body Politic. When Socrates was condemned for being right but offensively so, he was sentenced to commit suicide by taking hemlock. Plato's description of his dying may not be scientifically accurate by today's standards, but it describes the process; the poison gradually numbs the limbs 'til death. Good People, sometimes I have the feeling that's what I am witnessing; *tax Norquistism*—election after election is gradually poisoning the body Politic. It's got to stop, and you can do something about it this election.

Reagan did *many* good things as president, but he made raising taxes to pay for war the third or death rail in politics. Listen to Reagan-Bush and you can hear taps as the anti-Lincoln party lays the Grand Old Party to rest.

Fourth background. Conservatives believe in paying the costs of wars as they occur. That was plank one in the platform of the Lincoln we don't know (more soon). Not to be outdone, anti-Lincoln Republicans also say they believe in paying the costs of war, but for Heaven's sake not by raising revenues. What's wrong with you? No, the solution is to cut the quality and quantity of life for the empty sleeves. Never tax the god of Mammon, it seems to me, is the god Pat Robertson and Grover Norquist in their way genuflect to, at least that's the perception I feel they allow. "Raise taxes?" they smirk. "There's no need to increase revenues of a nation growing by approximately 100,000 million a decade or so. All we have to do is gut non-military discretionary spending on things like bridge upkeep, wetlands and clean water protection, food stamps, Head Start, Medicare and Social Security, job retraining, the autistic." The list grows long. But they blabber on: "Better the many go back to the hunter-gatherer days than raise taxes on the few 'producers.'"

Let me repeat that: *better the many go back to the hunter-gatherer days than raise taxes on "producers."* That outlook is killing conservatives today. "Hunker down, citizens of America," is the battle cry of Ryanomics. "Go back to the tired and weary days when your grandparents immigrated. Overlook the jobs and homes you lost in the latest Republican-ginned recession. Get a life." My point: the end of the Reagan Revolution is as bleak as the beginning was bright; unemployment and under-employment represents a return to hunter-gatherer days, doesn't it?

That's what the middle class is being reduced to, isn't it? To hunter gatherers with nomadic traits.

RANT #3

The Party of Lincoln

Every student I've taught has had an incomplete understanding of Abraham Lincoln. No fault of theirs; so did I until I began to rant about how the party of Lincoln has been twisted inside out to become the anti-Lincoln party.

Here's what I mean. Lincoln stood for five things we hear little, if anything, about. (1) Pay war debt. (2) Conciliation. (3) Compromise. (4) Amnesty. (5) Affirmative Action. Yep, exactly what the anti-Lincoln party today rejects.

We learn a lot about Lincoln growing up, but his truly conservative, original Republican values are scarcely mentioned. Let's go through these starting with Conciliation since we've touched on paying war debt already.

Conciliation: When Lincoln was nominated the first time, he had little if any choice over his vice-presidential running mate, a rabid abolitionist by the name of Hamlin. When he chose his running mate for a second term in 1864, he dumped the abolitionist and chose a slave owner. Yep; a slave owner. Talk about extending the hand of conciliation to the Confederacy . . . Andrew Johnson was a slave owner from a free state, Kentucky, and was able to keep his slaves after the Emancipation Proclamation because it applied only to states in rebellion (It took the 14th Amendment to free all slaves). Now get this: Johnson believed the rebellious states had a state's right to keep slavery as long as each wished—provided they rejoined the Union and did not demand extension into the territories west of Texas to the Pacific. Did Johnson come up with this "platform" on his own brilliance? No, it was Lincoln's idea, and Johnson, agreeing with him, was a main reason Lincoln chose him.

Although Lincoln detested slavery, he knew the tide of history was against slavery and envisioned its gradual elimination. England banned slave trade in the entire Empire in 1807, slavery itself in 1833. Several Latin and South American countries banned slavery during the early 1800s, and France banned it in 1851. (Twelve million slaves were "traded" into Latin and South America; four million into the United States; Brazil and Cuba were the last to outlaw slavery in the 1880s.)

One compromise made at the time the U.S. Constitution was written allowed the slave trade for another 20 years (until 1808); the South insisted upon it as a condition of ratifying the Constitution. During those 20 years, Congress passed over five laws restricting it (e.g., fined anyone building a ship meant for the slave trade; rewarded whistleblowers).

Lincoln read the historical tea leaves and preferred history, not war, end slavery in the United States. Talk about conservative principals; slow motion, molasses-like adaptation, let the "marketplace set the pace." (My phrase)

A second example of Lincoln's conciliatory stance was his (and General Grant's) policy of letting defeated Confederate troops surrender with honor (parade to stack arms) then take their rifles, horses and mules back to their farms (but officers not their pistols). *This was step one in rebuilding the economy of the south.* Y'all hear that: conciliation was step one in rebuilding the economy of the south. Grant notably did this after the long slugfest over Vicksburg, and then again at Appomattox when a defeated General Robert E. Lee, the hope of the Confederacy, surrendered.

A third example is seen in comparing Lincoln's terms for the rebellious states to rejoin the Union compared to the Republican Congress' terms. The Republican Congress took a severe accountability approach to the rebellious states; it was punitive in nature with tinges of vindictiveness. Congress insisted that 50% of eligible voters in each of the rebellious states had to sign a request for pardon in order for that state to be readmitted. Lincoln required only 10%. Politicking and horse trading went on like mad for sure, but it was Lincoln who chose the conciliatory approach. Another "Y'all hear": Lincoln intended his approach to speed the "healing" of the nation; the bringing of us together again. There's a message in there somewhere for Tea Partiers.

Compromise. The third of five key words to understanding the Lincoln you never knew is compromise (the first two were pay war debt and be conciliatory; the last two amnesty and affirmative action). Lincoln was opposed to slavery for many reasons, but he, as mentioned earlier, was amenable to its gradual extinction as history unfolded. Remember, he was a Republican, which meant he was a conservative, which meant he favored gradual, don't rock the boat, social adjustments. Secession rocked the boat and he was agin it with boots-dug-into-the-ground. Abolition, too, threatened to rock the boat if carried out "Now!" as abolitionists wanted. Lincoln's "end" was preservation of the Union; his "means" acceptance of slavery until the practice petered out. Let me rephrase that for emphasis. Lincoln was desirous by political philosophy to trade the good end Union for the most disagreeable means of continued slavery until it died out of what I call market forces. Slavery for another 10, 20, 40 or more years; the Lincoln we don't know was as much the Great Compromiser as he was the Great Emancipator we do know.

The key words are Big End/Uncomfortable Means. Today's "The deficit is ruining us" Loudmouths face a similar conundrum. The deficit could be reduced greatly if not eliminated altogether with an infusion of revenue, say a three-year graduated tax to war levels on everybody, poor and rich, including a "Victory Tax" earmarked exclusively for debt reduction. Presto, deficit no longer an issue *and America recaptures the tradition of solemn and inviolable obligation to pay accumulated war debt*, and Bonus, Bonus, Bonus, experiences a "We're in this together" moment. The means—increased revenue—would be particularly uncomfortable for the Loudmouths, but the end would be big and—Bonus, Bonus, Bonus—it would "bring us together" in common cause. Whoopee! To be Americans together again. This dual Lincoln-like opportunity is right there in front of the noses of the "No deficits, but no revenues either" crowd. All they have to do is reach out and touch the Lincoln we don't know. But will they? Shoot, who you kidding? Your answer is likely to be as good as mine.

In the four months between the time Lincoln was elected in November 1860 and his inauguration on March 4, 1861, seven states seceded; four more did after he was inaugurated. In his First Inaugural Address he said these lines we seldom if ever hear: "I have no purpose, directly or indirectly, to interfere with the institution of slavery in the States where it exists. I believe I have no lawful right to do so, and I have no inclination to do so." Many of us can recite parts of Lincoln's Gettysburg Address, but how many of us even knew he spoke these words: "I have no purpose, lawful right or inclination to interfere with slavery where it exists"? My point again is there is a Lincoln we know and a Lincoln we don't and the future of conservatism and the Republican Party is getting in touch with the one we don't know. The man knew how to prioritize values and understood means and ends and how to compromise over the highest of stakes.

Amnesty. Yep, the Lincoln we don't know stood for amnesty. A huge issue from the beginning to the end of hostilities was how to readmit the rebellious states. Jefferson Davis was as pro-Union as he was pro-slavery (he owned about 150 slaves) and opposed secession. He was a graduate of West Point, had served extremely well for 10 or more years in the U.S. Army, served four years as President Tyler's Secretary of War, and as Senator from Mississippi argued consistently and persistently for a Union half free, half slave (as opposed to Lincoln's famous "A nation divided against itself cannot endure.") When Mississippi seceded after Lincoln's inauguration, Davis followed suit and went off his rocker. By that I mean he not only advocated retention of slavery, but also the expansion of it to the Pacific Ocean (he had a political fit when California was admitted an entirely free state), and get this, he advocated *revival of the slave trade*. Talk about chasing old farts. Davis went from a reasonable sort as Senator opposed to secession to a radical as President of the Confederacy. (Look for similar traits among Tea Partiers.)

Throughout the long war an increasing number in the Planter class sought accommodation with the North, pressing for an armistice. They found agreement among some in the North. The McClellan wing of the Republican Party (yes, the General Lincoln fired) campaigned for armistice to the point where Lincoln's advisors thought the armistice crowd would defeat him in the 1864 election, and Lincoln prepared himself for what he, too, thought likely. Only several Grant victories turned the tide.

Let me rewind history for a moment. The Zealots at the time of Jesus were opposed to *any* compromise with the Romans—*any*—and the Romans responded in AD 70 by destroying much of Jerusalem, the Temple, the way the Jewish religion was conducted, and, of course, the Zealots. Smartasses might say the Zealots wrote the movie script for *Gone with the Wind.* By not compromising one iota, the Planter class took the Confederacy down for a 10 or knockout count.

Still, the deal Lincoln had proposed at the beginning of the war, he reissued near its end: each state in rebellion could continue with slavery as long as each chose, but there could be no expansion of it, and each state had to rejoin the Union. Lincoln was directly or indirectly privy to discussions of endorsing a constitutional amendment that guaranteed slavery in each state (talk about conciliation and compromise) as long as each chose to rejoin the Union. He also was party to discussion of paying slave owners for the "property" they lost as slaves were freed (He offered 15% of value for openers). Taken together, I submit these "platforms" represent more than conciliation; they represent some pretty serious tradeoffs: stay in the Union, keep your slaves.

Think about that; rejoin and keep slaves. Either Mississippi or Georgia, or both, or any other Confederate state could, under Lincoln's terms, have continued slavery for another 25, 50, 100 years. The heirs of plantation owners might have owned slaves in 1905 or 1965. I don't believe that for one moment, but you see the point; Lincoln was open to serious compromise, and Rebel refusal to strike a deal ended in the Rebels, like the Zealots, losing the whole enchilada. They risked everything to gain nothing. By insisting on "purity" and "compromise only over my dead body," they got their dead bodies, 258,000 of them across the 13 states of the Confederacy plus many more in Yankee territory. By putting "purity of position" and no compromising before common sense, they shot themselves in the groin (meaning the rebellious states lost a hell of a lot of fertile men, putting a crimp in recovery). It's called wrongheadedness, and one must ask has "new Georgia" or "new Mississippi" seen the darkness inherent in refusing to compromise when an advantageous deal is on the table (or mostly advantageous). If not, isn't it time for voters in both states to change their state's political colors and get with the program called democratic capitalism and it's march toward a Society of Dignity?

Lincoln understood pocketbook self-interest and knew how to work with those he disagreed with. No confederate state took him up on his offer although, as indicated, some considered doing so. Governor Vance of North Carolina vehemently opposed the idea and blew the confederate rendition of taps over the graves of 40,000 North Carolinians. What depths a person can go to in support of a wrong idea.

Let me ask a question. Does the Planter class' stance—all or nothing; purity of demand or we'll take the Union over the brink and into the abyss—

does that sound familiar? Aren't we hearing that nonsense from the anti-Lincoln party today; the party that pooh-poohs conciliation and scorns compromise? All or nothing was a poor choice then and it doesn't take an old poly sci professor to see that wrong choices foretell the future of the anti-Lincoln party.

Let me resume the narrative (and excuse any repetitiveness). Four years after his first inauguration and on the cusp of winning the Civil War, Lincoln did not need to be conciliatory or compromising. He did both. As Lee retreated from Richmond toward Appomattox, Lincoln even then offered each of the rebellious states a right to slavery where it existed (but not expanded) for as long as each state chose if they rejoined the Union. Lincoln read the winds of history correctly, one of the principal characteristics of conservatives (or at least it was). What is fresh to our understanding of Lincoln is that he was a compromiser willing to accept a most uncomfortable means in order to reach a superior end—preservation of the Union. It blows my "the Lincoln I know" mind to think the "Lincoln I didn't know" would put up with slavery for 10, 20 or more years, but he was a compromiser of the first order who realized the route to government of, by and for the people was circuitous.

Amnesty. How to readmit the rebellious states was a huge issue, as was what to do with the Planter class. Should their plantations, which had been divvied up and allocated to freed men, be confiscated permanently? Should members of the Confederate government be allowed to run for election? Enter the 10% rule mentioned earlier. If only 10% (not 50%) signed a request for pardon, the state could be readmitted. This meant the Planter class didn't have to beg if enough empty sleeves signed up. Additionally, Lincoln and his successor Andrew Johnson between them issued four amnesty declarations; the last included pardoning the remainder of the Planter class, including prisoner Jefferson Davis. Amnesty was a key platform in the Lincoln image of a Republican Party committed to conciliation, healing and unity and the progress that would follow. What's there not to understand about how the party of Lincoln has been replaced by the anti-Lincoln party? Reagan Democrats, it's time to come home.

Question: Lincoln's vision allowed 5.5 million rebellious confederates, many with guns aimed at your heart, to "immigrate back into" the Union (my phrase) after defecting and shooting 360,000 Yankees dead, so what's the hang-up about admitting 11 million unarmed *peaceful* immigrants? Oh, they're law breakers, you say. Well, shit, Confederates were, too, one far more than the other, wouldn't you say? How do you wrap your brain around the difference? I don't understand: let rebels "immigrate" back into the Union only to set up Jim Crow laws that turn full slaves into half slaves for another 100 years, and, by contrast fight tooth and nail against peaceful people like Raul Garcia who simply want to work their butts off putting fresh fruits and vegetables on Republican and Democrat dinner plates. With Jim Crow laws in place, what price did Rebels pay in ending the moral wrong of slavery? Why whoop and holler when Rebels wave their flag on the way to their voting precincts when Raul's immigrants don't have one to go to? Something is historically warped here. Okay, I know I'm on my soapbox, but let me ask: which is the more challenging, letting 5.5 million turncoats who shot at you or maybe killed your son "immigrate" back into citizenship for a second try, or letting 11 million nonviolent workaholics in for the first time?

Follow up question: Jesus was a notorious lawbreaker of civil, criminal and religious laws. A lawbreaker many times over, too. So, the Establishment Priests and politicos had him crucified for breaking the law and making outrageous claims (from their standpoint). Now, 2,015 years later we should crucify millions for peacefully breaking one law of no greater magnitude than any Jesus broke? I'm asking, just asking. Why crucify those who have been here for years, even decades? Why crucify settled immigrants even though they make no outrageous claims, go to church, maintain close families, would pay taxes if booked into the system, and have no interest in shooting you? Why crucify established immigrants for wanting a little piece of heaven on earth, as the Lord's Prayer inveighs? Have we learned nothing from Jesus' crucifixion that some feel it necessary to replicate it times millions? Christianity is a religion of suffering, not of beheading families; let established immigrants suffer through the hoops to legal citizenship, not crucify them. It's time to vote out CCC legislators—Caucasians Camouflaged as Christians—and elect Raul Garcias.

Garcia is an unknown farm worker who is challenging new House Minority Leader Kevin McCarthy in his agriculturally rich, dependent-on-immigrant-labor district for blocking comprehensive immigration reform. To use my terms, McCarthy has not been willing to accept uncomfortable means to achieve a meritorious end. Sharp as he is, and as badly in need of reform leadership as the Republican Party is, McCarthy seems trapped in an ideological time warp. He's not one to look forward to for Lincoln-like leadership. Is there, I ask, anyone in the Republican Party who is? I digress; back to the narrative.

The leadership I call the party of Lincoln stood for five things: pay war debts, conciliation, compromise, amnesty and . . . oh, yes, affirmative action.

Affirmative Action. I'm not bullshitting you. Lincoln stood for affirmative action. It wasn't called that; it was known as the Freedmen's Bureau, and it was a Peace Corp of its day. Lincoln initiated it, and it applies to the practice of politics: Mark 12:30-31 (love neighbor); Matthew 5:43 (love enemy); Romans 13:8-10 (love everybody) and Genesis 4:9-16 (Yes, you are your brother's keeper). There is no greater Lincoln political principal than this. The heart, soul and essence of the party of Lincoln is love neighbor, love enemy, love everybody, and yes, you are your brother's keeper. There's all the room in the world for wealth in this philosophy, in fact, there is a market for it, but to grasp the power in Lincoln's principle you have to ask Lyndon Johnson's question: what's the purpose of wealth? Some Republicans still gnaw their knuckles over that one.

Lincoln initiated and Congress passed the law creating the Bureau six weeks before Lincoln was assassinated. Its purpose was to facilitate the newly emancipated slave's transition to citizenship. The Freedmen's Bureau distributed rations to almost a million people (one fourth of whom were white empty sleeves), taught literacy, established schools, a judicial system, a contract labor system where the newly freed worked by contract with set pay rates rather than by chains, a land redistribution program for abandoned plantations, and similar initiatives.

Today we call this nation building; it's akin to what the U.S. has done after intervention in the Balkans, Iraq, Afghanistan, etc. It's a hell of a commitment, difficult to manage. We need only look at how the defeated Confederacy reacted to nation building. "Up yours" was the Planter's response when they regained power 12 years after the war. Given the choice between keeping traditional prejudices and becoming part of the movement of progressive societies, many—most—nearly all— Caucasians, masquerading as Christians, chose prejudices. In 1964 you could go from county to county across the old south and see which government forms the locals chose. You can still do that today, but the disguises of prejudice are more subtle and it must be clearly said, the positive effects of nation building are unambiguously evident. Big Government regulations that required affirmative hiring to win a federal contract to build parts for space vehicles, for example, gave the old south a choice between grits or big profits and some states and counties chose profits. Still, those who chose grits helped write the 2008 Republican Party platform that shrilled against social engineering and Big Government's attempt to control the individual and make him change his ways. What can you say? Chasing old farts is an art form for those who dislike nation building.

Back to 1865 and the Freedmen's Bureau. It was administered through the U.S. military and there was carpetbagger hanky-panky in the Bureau to be sure, but the Bureau was affirmative action loud and clear. It worked, too, and would have worked awesomely better had not the wasted Planter class fought against what they considered post-war military occupation. (There's a lesson here for the State Department and American foreign policy; our own vanquished said, "Get the Hell out. We don't want foreigners telling us how to live. We reject efforts to remake us and prefer to live as close as we can to the way we had been.") The Freedmen's Bureau lasted only until 1870-72, torpedoed by the Planter class as part of its march to regain control of the South. The election of 1876 resulted in four outcomes: it ended Union military presence in the discredited Confederacy; in exchange for ending that "occupation," the Planter class agreed to another four years of a Republican president (Rutherford B. Hayes) who tacitly agreed to let the Planter class have its way; it effectively elected Jim Crow across the South; and it substituted lynching for affirmative action.

Congress anticipated the latter; already in 1871 it passed the Ku Klux Klan Act authorizing military protection of blacks. The compromise of 1876 was the worst compromise Republicans made from an African American standpoint, and an unforgivable one. There is no Mark 12:30, Matthew 5:43, Romans 13:8-10, or and Genesis 4:9 in that compromise. Hayes' Republicans sold the freedman out. And 138 years later Republicans (at least the anti-Lincoln types) are still trying to keep the freedmen out. No one need ask why minorities vote Democrat; they know who has their back and who has a knife ready to plunge it in.

In today's language, Republicans who initiated the anti-Lincoln party threw African Americans under the bus. No wonder ever since they have voted Northern Lincoln-like Democrat and the confederate states Southern Jefferson Davis-like Democrat. Two trains going in opposite directions. After the Civil Rights Act of 1965 became law, ex-slave owning state voters seceded for a second time, this time from the Democratic Party and voted Republican, as earlier they had seceded from the Union. Twice in 100 years the "South" turned its back on the party of Lincoln, and I point this out to remind the State and Defense Departments that those who have been "invaded" don't change colors quickly. Nation building, even in America's "backyard," has taken time and more time and has cost more and more, and the pain for the entire body politic has been huge.

Digression: There is another teaching moment about affirmative action to capitalize on. It helps explain how the party of Lincoln transmogrified into the anti-Lincoln party. Affirmative action brings up an interesting question for Buchananists and their yell, "The non-European immigrants are coming, the non-European immigrants are coming. They'll never fit into melting pot America like immigrants particularly from northern Europe have. They breed like White Anglo-Saxon Protestants and Roman Catholics ought to and Caucasians Camouflaged as Christians are doomed in America. The non-European immigrant is coming."

This Satan-like bugle call causes citizens to be fearful, and FEAR has become the central emotion of the anti-Lincoln party. It stems partly from Pat Buchanan's 2002 *The Death of the West: How Dying Populations and Immigrant Invasions Imperil Our Country and Civilization.* His argument has merit statistically, great merit, but his interpretation of reality is right out of Chicken Little's "The sky is falling!" It has aroused fear in CCCs on a par with how Harriet Beecher Stow's, *Uncle Tom's Cabin,* aroused fear in Caucasian slave owners Camouflaged as Christians. We today are witnesses to how fear is playing out in the body politic and we claim to be a light to the world.

Buchanan's alarm about non-European immigrants outnumbering Caucasians by 2050 has spooked the White, Anglo-Saxon, Protestant and Roman Catholic voter. I have no way to know what

Buchanan's intent was; he's a studious, astute political observer who, I feel, simply reads history as going backward rather than forward. Intent aside, the effect of his rant has made FEAR the central emotion of today's anti-Lincoln party.

Let me mention this about fear and politics for a moment. Adolph Hitler in 1925 wrote in *Mein Kampf*, "[T]he weapon which most readily conquers reason [is] terror and violence." To which I add, both are preceded by fear and fear feeds them like gasoline feeds fire. As I rant elsewhere, democracy as we know it in the United States is a baby political experiment not three centuries old, and it is very fragile. There is no place in yours and my infant democracy for fear to be the unstated but controlling plank in a major political party's platform. As indicated, there are teaching moments in Confederate history: Fear of loss (of slavery) paralyzed the Planter class and led to self-destructive decisions; fear today can only lead to self-destructive decisions.

It was a CCC student in my American Government class who raised this question: "What was the largest non-European group to "invade" America?" Her answer: four million Africans brought to America against their will. Whether her numbers were accurate is open to discussion, but her point is well made. Years later now my question is, has the freed African American melted into the melting pot? He's tried mightily and succeeded (with some catching up to do) *despite* the 100 year denial of Freedmen Bureau-like affirmative action. The African American has been so successful despite the

"No Trespassing" signs he's encountered along the way that anti-Lincoln Republicans today have turned to voter suppression laws to "strain" them out of the melting pot as if they were flies in gumbo. Thom Tillis, North Carolina state Republican house speaker and candidate for Senate, is a poster boy for voter suppression. He is so entrenched and backed by big money he is an example of why I believe return to a party of Lincoln is going to require Reagan Democrats to return to the Democratic Party for a cycle or two. At least until the anti-Lincoln party people are flushed out of the system like bad apples from the intestines.

Once given the yellow caution light, African Americans have done their damndest to melt in and would have melted more if not given the red light by some. The great lesson—listen up now—the great lesson the Afro-American has taught us is immigration in America works when allowed to, even for those kept in moral handcuffs and, yes, chains. End long digression.

Back to the last of Lincoln's five attributes, affirmative action. The Freedmen's Bureau ended after only six-seven years when the hugely white Christian south circled their wagons and replaced affirmative action with Jim Crow "black code" laws, making it illegal for newly freed slaves to sign a contract, testify against whites, marry whites, keep land, even be unemployed, etc., and Lord help them if they were caught puzzled and wandering in the maze of freedom trying to figure things out—grounds to be jailed for loitering.

After the Civil War, Union states went on to thrive while CCC ruled confederate states loitered their way in a slow shuffle. It's only opinion, but I feel the lingering portion of the "old south" still prefers shuffle, if not backwards. Still, I'm optimistic. Some mornings I read the paper and say, Well dadgum, a few of them dudes in state capitols like Tallahassee, Atlanta, Montgomery and Richmond (well, maybe not Richmond) asking, "Foreword? What's that?" Still, I have to add this: North Carolina's 1954-1961 progressive governor Luther Hodges is rotating in his grave like a pig on a spit since the anti-Lincoln Thom Tillis voter-suppression party now in Raleigh has taken to passing newfangled black codes. Oh, they don't call them that, but this is a moment for the Shadow: "Who knows what evil lurks in the hearts of old fart chasers?" I feel "Uncle Thom Tillis" uses the euphemism progress or some such as a comforting word to cover for fearful Caucasians Camouflaged as Christians.

Lincoln talked the talk and walked the walk of war debt repayment, conciliation, compromise, amnesty and affirmative action. Now, using the fingers on one hand, how many of these five do Loudmouth Tea Partiers stand for? Hold up your clenched fists. See, that's why I refer to them as the anti-Lincoln Party.

Let me cite an example of the impact the Planter-anti-Lincoln mentality has had on wages in our day. Question: After more than 250 years of slavery, do you really expect a legislator from a slave state, like Thom Tillis, to vote for a minimum wage? Are you nuts? Slavery and minimum wage doesn't compute. There is no DNA linkage at all. Similarly, trying to morph slave ownership into acceptance of labor unions is like trying to breed cats and giraffes; it's not going to happen. Lastly, draw me the distinction between Planter class mentality and Corporations are people in disguise, have free speech rights and can do with their money and workers damn near anything the slave owners used to be able to do. Where's the distinction?

To bring conclusion to this rant, in Major Rant #1, I sought to initiate a discussion about how the party of Lincoln (what once was known as the Grand Old Party) transmogrified into the anti-Lincoln, what's-in-it-for-me party. President Ronald Reagan deserves acknowledgment for his accomplishments, and I do respect those many accomplishments. Still, as we live into the aftershocks of the Reagan Revolution, we see better an aspect of his philosophy that accelerated the arrival already underway of the anti-Lincoln party. I feel this one aspect of Reagan as President represents another step in the killing of the Republican Party.

In this Rant I've introduced the Lincoln we didn't know, the five pillars of wisdom he stood for (pay war debt, conciliation, compromise, amnesty and affirmative action), and the anti-Lincoln party's rejection of every one of those pillars.

Now, go vote.

RANT #4

Debt History

A brief review of war debt history may explain why I feel a touch of sarcasm is warranted. "During most of America's wars, parochial desires—such as tax breaks for favored groups or generous spending for influential constituencies—have been *sacrificed* to the greater good," Robert Hormats tells us in *The Price of Liberty: Paying for American Wars* (Italics mine). "Sacrifice?" Yes, that's the word Hormats uses. Long time no hear, eh?

Lincoln and others in the Union believed in taxation sacrifice; they considered payment of war debt "sacred and inviolable" and made the point by passing the 14th Amendment which made the Union's income tax constitutional (above legal challenge). The 14th Amendment represents "the constitutionalization of sacrifice" (my wordy term meaning the enshrining of tax sacrifice as a Constitutional value). The 14th also represents traditional values. President Reagan: "There is a mandate to impose a voluntary return to traditional values." Nicely said; he talked the talk, but his budgets didn't walk the walk. Deficits ballooned into Big Government with little suggestion of a "sacred and inviolable" obligation to pay Star Wars debt (which led to the axing of the budget for the autistic). When today's Republicans talk about deficit reduction you have to peek behind the Oz curtain to see if they include taxation sacrifice among the Constitutional values they preach us to return to. Certainly President "Duh" Bush didn't have a clue. Question: you look at Republican presidents since Eisenhower and you wonder who has contributed to the killing of the Republican Party?

Prior to the Civil War debts were paid pretty much on a pay as you fight basis by raising tariffs or excise taxes, not by taxing incomes. Now listen to this: both the Union and the Confederate States of America levied income taxes during the Civil War. The Union income tax, the first ever, was no tax under $600 of income, 3% on $600 to $10,000, 5% to $50,000, over that 7.5%. Confederate taxation was a *Saturday Night Live* laugh; there was no established infrastructure for collection, and would you believe (hold your sides to keep from splitting) the plantation owners objected to Jefferson Davis centralizing power in Richmond, as Lincoln was doing in Washington for the Union. It's one of the most ironical moments in U.S. history; they went to war to defend states' rights against a centralized power telling them what to do and by damn if they were willy-nilly going to give up their state's right to a Confederate central government demanding money and men for openers. Davis had to herd the 13 states like the proverbial herd of cats. Talk about not thinking things through ahead of time. Miscalculation remained one of the southern states biggest problems for over 100 years and the hangover lingers.

Isn't it oxymoronic to say "Let's fight, but not centralize?" Isn't it equally oxymoronic for today's anti-Lincoln party to screech, "Let's fight, but not tax?"

You white folk who have concentrated yourselves in the suburbs and vote Republican for a variety of reasons, can't you see how "Let's fight, but not centralize" and "Let's fight, but not tax" has shredded the sacred and inviolable value of tax sacrifice proclaimed by the Founding Fathers, endorsed by the party of Lincoln and enshrined in the Fourth Article of the 14th Amendment, and has led to the anti-Lincoln party? You can put a stop to it if you can accept what I consider conclusive—that the Reagan Revolution included an egocentric tax philosophy of ME before the nation that has created a culture of *tax Norquistism* that is hurting the United States of America as well as you.

One of the great ironies of the Civil War is the slave owning states trying to preserve states' rights by centralizing power in Richmond with Jeff D as honcho. (See *Tax History Museum* for interesting overview.) One of the great ironies of today is the Republican Party trying to preserve Everyman's rights by centralizing power in the few mighty wealthy with the Koch brothers as honchos.

As indicated, the Union considered payment of

war debt "sacred and inviolable" and made that point Constitutional by passing the 14th Amendment. On the other hand, winners set terms for losers and all Confederacy debt was repudiated. So much for losers losing their money to a losing cause; they also lost property they called slaves and 258,000 confederate lives. I call attention to this trifecta of losses only to illustrate what price believers in a losing cause will pay. It would be naïve not to expect the anti-Lincoln, anti-tax party to fight rather than switch. Like the Confederacy tried with the Union, they have already tried to take America down by ruining the full faith and credit of the nation. Extremism in the defense of nonsense is a vice and it's killing the G.O.P.

World War I saw the U.S. debt rise from $74.2 million to $18.9 *billion*, a 2,459% increase. Congress didn't dodge the bullet: it levied surtaxes up to 77% on incomes, established a permanent estate tax and a war-profits tax on corporations. WWI also marks a huge change in how war debt was financed; not only by taxes mentioned above, but also by borrowing money (largely from the wealthy) by the selling of bonds through the Liberty Bond Act promoted by Woodrow Wilson (bonds allow for an orderly repayment of debt). Eleven surpluses during the 1920s reduced debt by a third. The sacred and inviolable obligation to pay war debt down, if not off, still held. (Side comment: Despite the huge cost of WWI, Congress passed the Veterans Bonus Bill to pay soldiers for lost wages, but Republican presidents Harding and Coolidge vetoed similar veterans' bills. Republicans talk war tough, but who's got your back veterans?

Things get a little dicey beginning with the Great Depression. It brought about a huge loss of revenue when the marketplace created (or allowed, your choice) the collapse of the economy, and then failed for four years under Hoover to generate a solution. (Create a problem, fail to solve it; this party deserves your vote? Just asking.) FDR's ten-year-long attempt to bail poor and rich alike out of desperate trouble was attempted through the New Deal (when the market fails, government steps in and helps, like a sober brother helping an alcoholic brother gone woozy). FDR had one advantage that Hoover did not have; Hitler's rise to power caused a massive flow of capital out of Europe into investments in the U.S. Ah, the miracles that revenue can produce; the inflow of foreign revenue helped bring about a small budget surplus by 1937.

The economy was well on its way to recovery when a decision with fateful consequences was made; the historical distaste of debt and the tradition of paying debt down led to money being prematurely pulled out of the economy and the nation fell into a second recession—the infamous 1937-38 "recession within a depression." The two-fold lesson: when a drunken Big Marketplace falls in the gutter, federal government must step in with a 12-step program to help the alcoholic up; and second, step in wholeheartedly, but withdraw gradually. In Fast and Big, out Slow and Easy. It's really not so complicated that an anti-Lincoln Republican can't understand the importance of revenue to government when a nation is in crisis. It's like a blood transfusion to a G.I. whose legs have been blown off—it's a lifesaving action.

WWI led to the maximization of borrowing through bonds to supplement taxation as a way to pay war debt. How, then, to pay for the humongous debt incurred in WWII? Four steps: broaden the tax base to include 50 million more citizens, limit private consumption through rationing, sell War Bonds like mad, and (keep your senses now) increase war time taxes to the 90% rate. That rate, you will recall, led movie actor Reagan to avoid high war time taxes by taking a powder rather than make another movie.

I harp on this point for a reason. The concept I call *tax citizenship* has been responsible for the payment of war debt since the founding of the nation. Adopting Alexander Hamilton's philosophy, the new federal government assumed the Revolutionary War debt of each of the states; talk about bellying up to the bar of responsibility.

The words *tax citizenship* are not in the founding documents or *The Federalist*, but tax citizenship is in the DNA of the Declaration of Independence and the Constitution. It expects sacrifices on the home front in proportion to the sacrifices made by limping, empty sleeves. It includes post-war veteran benefits, too; Lincoln and Grant, for example, allowing defeated Confederate soldiers to take their rifles and mules home. *Tax citizenship* isn't hard to grasp, is it? So what's gone wrong? Where did the train leave the tracks? Who is accountable?

Tax citizenship, dear friends, it what true conservatism means; accountability and responsibility and sacrifice, yes sacrifice for the greater good. Lincoln walked that walk, but somewhere well before Reagan the Republican Party stopped walking and started babbling nonsense. Still, I submit, actor Reagan going A.W.O.L. to avoid high war time taxes while others died on beachheads has become a philosophical-political role model that has legitimized others trashing the 200 year tradition of *tax citizenship*. Replaced by what? Replaced by what I call *tax Norquistism* or the minimization of *tax citizenship* to the point of mockery. President Reagan: "There is a mandate to impose a voluntary return to traditional values." Which traditional values? Family values I see and feel in President Reagan's speeches, *tax citizenship* I don't. In fact, rather than a mandate to return to a fundamental component in our Constitutional DNA, I see and feel Reagan's fellow accumulators of Big Money volunteering not to sacrifice on behalf of *tax citizenship*, but to sign on to *tax Norquistism*. A person making wealth in America and taking it to a foreign country to avoid *tax citizenship* is an example of *tax Norquistism*. "Make here, steal it away there," like moving corporate headquarters to a foreign nation to avoid taxes is another example not of *tax citizenship*, but of *tax Norquistism*. A third example is launching CCWs, Credit Card Wars. The latter is a total repudiation of the concept of *tax citizenship*.

Again my argument: *Tax citizenship* is as much a part of the DNA of our constitutional documents as freedom of religion. Or at least it was. Alexander Hamilton would be the first of the Founding Fathers to upchuck in their graves over CCWs.

Tax Norquistism is more than objection to a specific tax or taxation in general. It has become a philosophy. An ethos. A cultural value. It is based on three premises as I see it. First, taxation is a psychological evil; it represents power to dictate command and control the individual. *Power, not taxes, is the real issue undergirding tax Norquistism.* Second, a nation of 317 million can be governed in the same way a nation of 3.9 million was in 1789. Third, morality does not progress; the elderly Mr. and Ms. Everyman of the 21st century are condemned to live like the elderly in the 18th century.

Let's look at these three elements further. Power, the so-called narrowing of freedom, is the political psychology undergirding *tax Norquistism.* According to *tax Norquistism* taxation has nothing to do with revenue; revenue is only a by-product. Rather, taxation has everything to do with *oppressing the individual.* This from the 2008 Republican Economic Platform: "Today's Democratic Party views the tax code as a tool of social engineering. They use it to control our behavior, steer our choices and change the way we live our lives. Taxes, by their very nature, reduce a citizen's freedom." Well, there you are. Taxes aren't the problem; they're only a symptom of what's loathsome. It's your precious Egocentric ME being violated that's at the heart of the anti-tax movement. Power, not revenue, is the issue; psychology, not economics is where to look for the cause of the malady.

We're closer to "Everyman is an island" than to "No man is an island." Indulge in John Donne's poem with me: "No man is an island, Entire of itself, Everyman is a piece of the continent, A part of the main . . . ." This argument has being going on since cavemen fought over bones, but that's no excuse for us. Our Founding Fathers gave us a recipe for solving that conundrum. They called it sacrifice for the general good; I call it *tax citizenship*.

Compare these two sentences. First, Mr. and Ms. Everyman: "Of course we prefer to keep as much of the money we earn as we can." Second: "Taxes control our behavior, steer our choices and change our lives." The psychological difference between these two frames the clash of civilizations that pits one American against another.

Compare these two sentences made by movie stars. First: "[I] always chose to 'loaf' around rather than make more than two pictures a year. Why should I have done a third picture, even if it was *Gone with the Wind?* What good would it have done me?" Second: "I was glad to [pay $300,000 in federal taxes on $465,000 of income.] Income tax money all goes into improvement and protection of the country." Again I submit, the difference between these two mindsets frames the clash of civilization that is ripping the country of our Founding Fathers apart like the curtain of the Holy of Holies was rent at the moment of Jesus' death. (Matthew 27:51) It's serious, Good People. It's serious. And you can do something about it in the voter's booth this coming election. Now.

"What good would it have done me to be in *Gone with the Wind?*" puts forward the notion actor Reagan put money before fame. Just think, a smartass colleague suggested, "If he'd starred in that movie, he might not have had to make *Bedtime for Bozo.*" I consider that a snide remark, but his point was that Reagan as an actor had undecided values.

The declaration, "Taxes go to the improvement and protection of the country," was made in 1937 by zany movie star Carole Lombard. Her way of thinking left her with take home pay of $2,705,000 in 2014 dollars, with $4,918,000 going to help the country out of the Great Depression. The Founding Fathers thought of it as putting the country first; that's how the Revolutionary War debt was paid in little over a decade. Why, despite the War of 1812, the national debt was eliminated by 1840 (Well, $11,000 comes close to eliminated). Why the Korean War did not add a penny to the debt. Why Lyndon Johnson called for tax increases to defer the costs of the Vietnam War. I call this a first order of business value.

Carole Lombard's second husband was Clark Gable; they honeymooned in Oatman, Arizona, and if you have never been to this mining "camp" on old Route 66, do so; you're in for a hoot. Forty days after Pearl Harbor, Carole Lombard became an empty sleeve. No, worse than that—she died in a plane crash returning to Hollywood after raising $2 million in a war bond drive in her home state of Indiana. That's $32 million in 2014 dollars raised 40 days after Pearl Harbor. Carole Lombard was one of this country's first citizen victims of World War II.

One other "actor" contrast to make: Ann Sheridan, the "Oomph Girl" and pin-up actress throughout World War II said, "I regret that I have only one salary to give my country." She appeared in two movies with Ronald Reagan, including the one he thought his best, *Kings Row*. Was her comment "only one salary to give" a dig at Reagan for double dipping—military plus Big Money movie pay? I doubt it, but the question is there to be answered. A list of movie folks she mentioned in interviews included Error Flynn, James Cagney, John Garfield, Betty Davis, Jack Warner, and Cary Grant, but not Ronald Reagan. It's worth pointing out, too, that Sheridan's "I regret I have only one salary to give for my country" has a resounding patriotic tone to it; it's a takeoff on Nathan Hale's "I only regret, I have but one life to lose for my country." [Hale, a spy for the colonies in revolt against the King, was captured by the British and executed.]

I harp on this issue for a reason. I reiterate that Ronald Reagan was a decent person and a good President. Still, once the curtain of Oz is pulled aside what do we see? The long term impact his philosophy of "Big Money men quit work and go to the country to loaf when their taxes get too high" has directly and indirectly become a code of life, a cultural value that has infected the body Politic with two fatal diseases: income maladjustment on the everyday practical level and *tax Norquistism* on the philosophical.

Lest you think I'm coming down hard on America, 'tain't true. Read the next Rant.

RANT #5

History's Lesson: From Hardscrabble Poor to Wealth to *Gone with the Wind*

History is a mean teacher. By mean I mean demanding, exacting, always remorseless. It's like an odd antique; you can hide it but you can't get it out of your family history. You either put it on the mantel to admire or you put it in the attic where it haunts your dreams. Either way you can't escape the lessons of history.

One is this: nations that start out hardscrabble and pioneering become wealthy, develop plastic ethics particularly at the higher levels, become hubristic, then replace the values that made them great with garbage. It's the trajectory that describes empires. Plato and Aristotle did not write to promote democracy in classical Athens; they wrote after the barn burned down; after Athens had speared itself in the foot by becoming an imperial war power that miscalculated and lost at Syracuse and then Sparta. They wrote to figure out what in hell went wrong and propose remedies.

Gibbon's *Decline and Fall of the Roman Empire*

traces the same pattern: from grub stake to wealth to plastic ethics (think Nero) and decline. Will and Ariel Durant's encyclopedic, *Story of Civilization*, highlights this reality: start poor, get rich, go to pieces. Arnold Toynbee's histories confirm this, too. Most recently Ari Shavit in his insightful history of Israel traces the same pattern: pioneering Israel with a farmer's ethics transmogrifying into hubris with 100 nuclear weapons to back up its policy of expansion through settlements. His beautifully written book is *My Promised Land: The Triumph and Tragedy of Israel.* I, too, have used this pattern or trajectory as a leitmotiv of my 2009 book, *Damn the Warocracy: A Plea to Restore American Democracy,* and in my just published (August 2014) *A Global Architecture of Survival: Lessons from the Jewish Experience.*

I cite these histories (there are dozens of others) to make this point: America, the country we love, is not immune from this trajectory in history. In an amazingly short period of time we have, by diligent effort and disciplined thinking, worked ourselves through the initial hardscrabble period, and we now are at a tipping point where the spirit of discovery and invention is being countered by a spirit of plastic ethics which somehow always follows the accumulation of wealth. In America as I write, plastic ethics is seen foremost in the downgrading of *tax citizenship* and the promotion of *tax Norquistism.*

Again, I'm not picking on America in this book of rants; I'm just pointing out the historical trend that has swallowed up previous successful nations. The decision is yours to make, Good People, each time you go into a voter's booth. Which disposition is yours? To vote for plastic ethics that only the wealthy can afford to indulge, like "I prefer to loaf than pay high taxes." Or is your disposition this election to vote for "I regret I have only one salary to give for my country?"

There's time for corrective action. Come home to the party that values Contract but sees it as a means to a Society of Dignity.

RANT #6

Who Are the Tea Partiers
Really Mad At?

Self-disclosure: I was *almost* 100% with the original Tea Party advocates largely because they seemed to stand for *tax citizenship*, regretted they had only one paycheck to give for their country, didn't seem egocentric, and initially were spot on about whom they were mad at: George W. Bush. Why not? During his eight years the national debt grew by $4.9 trillion. That's enough to panic any voter, but what really provoked anger was President Bush's "Why care?" attitude and the nation had little to show for it: failed wars in Afghanistan and Iraq, huge bailout of Wall Street, Main Street thrown under the bus, nine million jobs lost, and $19.2 trillion lost in household wealth. If you were not Mr. or Ms. Everyman at the time, put yourself in their shoes. I submit $19.2 trillion lost in household wealth alone was enough to make them ANGRY. It did me. (45% has been recovered with the economic upswing; some much more, a few 110%.)

The drift toward anger had been building throughout the Bush years, but the stroke that broke the voter's trust was the Financial Crisis at the end of Bush's time as President. Lucky Bush, the crisis erupted in late 2008 and he suffered for only a few months (half of January, December, November, October) and then he was out of there. He turned tail for Texas to hide out at the ranch like cattle thieves of yesteryear hid out in the Palo Duro Canyon near Amarillo. Who was left in Washington to manage the crisis and take the blame? Guess.

Another way to highlight who the Original Tea Partiers were mad at is to compare Hoover-Roosevelt with Bush-Obama. We know Obama inherited a Bush contrived economic disaster. We know he threw himself under the Bush bus for the benefit of the nation. Obama put his presidency as a sacrifice on the altar of bailing the nation out of Bush's Great Recession, while killjoys bellowed to see his birth certificate.

Here's what I mean. Herbert Hoover was elected in November 1928, and took office in March '29. Seven months later the Gilded Age crashed on his head, in October. He had more than three years before the next election to fix the catastrophe. He failed, largely because he thought that "locals" should take care of the poor, the hungry and the unemployed (sound familiar?). Never mind if all experience said otherwise; ideology ruled. Hoover, by all accounts, was a good guy and great organizer. Still, I imagine his attitude went something like this: "You don't adjust plans to fit circumstances; you force circumstances to fit plans." (That's a reverse quote from General George Patton who believed success depended upon adjusting plans to fit circumstance.) In effect, Hoover was telling failing local and state governments since taking care of the locals was historically a local matter, state and country governments need to tax more to take care of the locals. It's a classical example of don't change outdated ideology to fit new and unimaginable circumstances; damn-it change the circumstances to fit the ideology. It is a fundamental difference between the Democratic and the present Republican parties (It wasn't always that way). It's also the stance the Confederate or slave states took resulting in war.

More Hoover-like thoughts: Despite the suffering of so many, despite the states, cities and towns going downhill fast and flirting with bankruptcy, they should up their taxes and the natives should up their charity in the name of providing for the General Welfare and assuring Domestic Tranquility. No nationwide systemic problem is too big for farmers to solve. Don't you remember the greatness of rural America in the 18th and 19th centuries when more than 70% of the U.S. population lived in rural areas? Back when people knew and took care of one another, like they did in West Branch, Iowa, where Hoover was born and raised; or Tampico, Indiana, where Reagan was born and raised?

Hoover was "Good Riddanced" out of office in the next election, but the "Let the locals take care of charity" mentality continues to haunt the Republican

Party as Marley's ghost haunts Scrooge.

Four years of Hoover's "make circumstances fit ideology" went by before Franklin Delano Roosevelt was nominated in 1932 as the Democratic candidate for the presidency. (Don't get me wrong. Hoover had a few good ideas but too little and too late.) During those four years FDR had nothing to do with Hoover's struggles; he did not link any part of his strategy to Hoover's failed efforts. That's why we talk of Hoover in terms of the Great Depression and FDR in terms of innovative Recovery. The calendar made sure the full weight of the Great Depression fell on Hoover's desk. When Roosevelt took office in March 1933, he immediately set to adjusting plans to fit the circumstances of the Great Depression. Untainted by Hoover's mentality—his adjusted plans worked. (Slowly to be sure, in part because the economic hole the nation had fallen into was harder to get out of than Daniel his den; in part because a Supreme Court wedded to old ideology rebuffed him case after case.)

Poor Obama. He had been nominated and was campaigning, but was still a month from being elected when the Financial Crisis burst like a piñata whacked by a millionaire before jumping. FDR had four years to let the blame settle squarely on Hoover; Obama had three months. His presidency was about to begin and the need was obvious—he had to have a say in whatever resolutions were cobbled together because he would have to manage them. The calendar worked *against* Hoover and *for* FDR; it worked *for* Bush, *against* Obama. Unlike FDR,

Obama didn't really have a choice; he could have kept a 100-mile distance between Bush's spiraling out of control administration and his. Instead several months before his inauguration he chose to put his presidency at risk, and like a good *tax citizen* put the nation's interest first. (And the ne'er-do-wells wanted to see his birth certificate. Somebody needs to get a life.)

Bush escaped tar and feathering like a rat escapes a barn flooding with water. Obama took the hit. After two years of managing the mess that Bush's failures dumped on him, abetted by Republican foot dragging, it was not Bush or Republicans, but Obama and Democrats who paid the price in the 2010 midterm elections. That election turned on one key factor—both Original and Angry-but-Confused Tea partiers lost sight of who they were really mad at.

The Loudmouths seized the opportunity like a starved snake a mouse. This is where transference comes in. Let me put it this way: Bush was the arsonist who fled, Obama the fireman who stayed to put the fire out, and the public blamed the fireman. The best that can be said is this: the Greeks called it Fate. It was unfortunate for President Obama and disaster for the nation.

Why disaster? The depths of the recession, and the drawing out of it as far as possible by Republicans, gave Big Business time to experiment with employment practices. Layoffs, demanding more productivity from fewer employees, part-time employees, temporary employees, hiring through temp agencies, vetoing pay raises, downloading cost of benefits onto employees, computers to screen applications rather than seeing prospects live (leaving the applicant demoralized and confused about how to job hunt), and oh, oh, oh, preferring not to invest in employees but in technologies. Remember the adage, "Go home with the person you brought to the dance?" Well, employees helped bring employers to the dance, but now employers started going home with robots.

On the streets it's known as "The screwing of the American Worker," but like rape there is nothing the worker wants to remember about the screwing. Yeah, I understand businesses got to do what they got to do, but my point is this: the depth, swath and length of the Great Recession, abetted by foot dragging Republicans, gave employers time and more time and still more time to experiment with employment practices until the employment marketplace was turned inside out. It simply isn't the same as it was five years ago.

Heads up: this change in the nature of employment has had as major an impact on the work place as has the shipment of jobs overseas with equally long-term consequences. The employment face of America is changing and it's a critical part of why employment and pay have remained stagnant while the economy generally is rebounding. Yes, I'm saying the size of Bush's disasters, Republican delays and half-measures, and Loudmouth antics have led to fundamental changes in the employment economy.

Good People, the circumstances have changed. New plans are necessary. Middle-management and ol' callused hands are dazed and wondering where they fit in society now. We're talking major social reorganization that will take decades to work through. My belief is the employment marketplace of America 2040 won't look like that of America 1945, the beginning of a three-decade-long prosperity happening that included the Great Society, precursor to a Society of Dignity. It makes me ask, "Have I lived at the height of American civilization?" It's been a great ride I'll tell you that.

Three paraphrased quotes from Hitler's *Mein Kampf*: "Limit propaganda to a few points, devised exclusively for the masses, and drive them into their skulls with indefatigable persistence." (185) Second, "Fear is the weapon which most readily conquers reason." (41.) Third, "[B]y clever and persevering use of propaganda even heaven can be represented as hell to the people." (276) Any of these tactics sound familiar as you listen to today's Republican Party advertisements?

Apply that last choice morsel to what the Loudmouth Tea Partiers have done to the Fireman working to put out the fire started by Bush. I don't think it was by accident they chose to represent the nation's heavenly time with its first minority president as hell. Using mental graffiti they have taken the hope and promise of that breakthrough election and turned the nation's moment of Heaven into Hell.

Are you really considering voting for these fear

mongers and cruise missiles again?

Do you recall the statue of Saddam Hussein being pulled down? The statue of Stalin torn down? Or Lenin's? That's what the Loudmouth Tea Partiers and the leadership of the Republican Party in the House and Senate have tried to do—tear down one of the great moments in American history. They had a choice—they could have built on the moment but instead, they chose to destroy it. This is another example of what I mean by the party of Honest Abe has been replaced by the anti-Honest Abe Party.

Despicable. All because the Tea Partiers forgot who they were really mad at and let the Loudmouths take over. Sad, but there's time to recover in the voting booth next time you enter.

RANT #7

The Myth of the Gilded Age

If you don't understand the current Republican theory of economic growth, you won't be able to see why the party is in its death-throes.

It's a theory, all right, and one that has proven to redistribute wealth *upward* in dramatic fashion (socialism for the few), straining and shrinking the middle class, and strangling the lower-classes, forcing them to rely on government aid. And all the while the Republicans insist on slashing that aid, starving the beast, to "motivate" the helpless poor. In other words, it's a sure-fire, dead-ender for progress. Pretty perverse, huh?

We've covered this theory already. Remember "trickle-down"? Reaganomics? Yeah, that firmly discredited idea, again. Most Republican thinkers no longer dare to use these words, but there's little doubt they still adhere to the theory. How else to justify Bush's massive tax cuts for the richest Americans? Admitting that these vaunted economic theories were dead wrong in the effects they produced would bruise too many fragile egos, it seems. Instead, Republican thinkers have to attempt to rewrite history.

Just because the population of the United States has grown from 4 million in 13 colonies along the eastern seaboard in 1787, to 315 million in 50 states from sea to shining sea today, well, that's no call for growth in ideas, is it? And just because cultural and ethnic diversity has increased a thousand-fold since 1787, that's no reason to think any differently about how society ought to work and where people fit in it, right? And, well, just because scientific and technological advances have revolutionized how economies work since the Industrial Revolution, that's no very good reason to rethink how economies should function, right? Of course not, it's the fundamentals, stupid.

Stupid is as stupid does. Yes, yes, I know, conservative by definition means holding the line on the *status quo*. I know. But holding the line on the *status quo* never meant ignoring reality—and it never meant rejecting growth. In the political and social sense, conservatisms' job is to slow down and think through and rationalize change—which is admittedly inevitable—so that chaos is kept at bay; conservatism isn't supposed to deny and hide from change—which creates a whole different kind of chaos. A true conservative understands that things change, and he wants to make the best of that change, so he goes at it and attempts to channel it in safe and sane directions, maintaining what is good from the past, but also selecting what is good from the present and supporting it. A true conservative, for example, when the evidence for global warming becomes undeniable, says to himself, "all right, we've got a problem, and something has got to change."

I have never considered Paul Ryan to be qualified by experience for the Presidency. Recently, he blew himself out of the water when he voiced his doubts about man-made climate change. His dismissive attitude toward 99% of scientific opinion damns him, it seems to me. I'd rather have Joe Schmo, who didn't graduate 6th grade, be president than someone who can dismiss a majority scientific opinion with an idiot phrase like "the climate always changes." Ryan is a perfect example of one ailment that undercuts Republican thought: he suffers from the "boggle threshold." This is the level above which the mind boggles when faced with some new fact or report or idea. The fact of human-caused climate change and the dangers it presents simply boggle the poor man's feeble little ideology. He's trying to make lemonade out of the climate change lemons, but the Party is already full of stupid loudmouth know-nothings that need something stiffer than lemonade.

So, what does the current "conservative" party say when faced with overwhelming evidence of global climate change and its dangers? It says "hoax!" That's bubble-culture and boggle threshold if there ever was such a thing. How can Republican thinkers and politicians—folks who are mostly business-persons, lawyers, stockbrokers, smart enough people but not climate scientists themselves—how can they call the conclusions of 99% of climate scientists a hoax? The answer is easy, if a bit cynical—money. Mammon, again. The fossil fuel industries—all of them, oil, coal (there's no such animal as "clean" coal—that's a pure fraud), natural gas, etc.—need climate change to be a hoax in order to keep their profits up, and to hell with our grandkids; and, as Will Rogers famously said, "America's got the best politicians money can buy." There's no big mystery here.

Incidentally, Obama's climate change record is pretty dismal—damn dismal, in fact, and this is one big reason for his low approval ratings; he has badly betrayed his base supporters on environmental issues—so money talks pretty loud to both parties, although you won't hear Democrats calling climate change a hoax.

Back to this notion of growth and change in ideas. Growth and change is what liberals (Democrats) do. It's a necessary service they provide for society and the nation. Conservatives (Republicans) are there to slow and channel that growth and change, to prevent the potential chaos that rapid or wrong change can create. Also a necessary service they provide. Both sides of this political scale are necessary for a healthy democratic society—and ideally they would balance nicely, right in the middle.

The trouble today is, the two sides have flip-flopped—or at least the terminology has. Today Republicans are the liberals, pushing for rather dramatic changes and going backwards, and the Democrats are the conservatives, attempting to put the brakes on and rationalize that change.

Bosh! That's preposterous! What mean ye?

Today's Republican agenda is clearly to return America to a pre-FDR Gilded Age; this means no more Social Security and Medicaid, no more unemployment insurance, no more federal aid for poor or disadvantaged (let the church provide those services, just like back then—wink-wink); and it means that industry is almost entirely free to do as it chooses—especially the financial industry. It means no more consumer protection, no guarantees that the food you buy is fit to consume or the water from your tap is clean, no guarantees that the job you do will be safe, and no guarantees that if you do get hurt at work you won't simply be tossed out on your ass to fend for yourself. It means all of this and much more, far too vast to survey here. This is an agenda for radical change, and it's a hell of a distance from maintaining the *status quo*.

In April of 2011, the Republican majority in the House of Representatives passed legislation that would have shrunk the percentage of federal non-defense discretionary spending to Pre-Great Depression levels. The country is a much bigger and more complicated place today than it was in 1928. We've had all kinds of history to learn from in the past 85 years. But these crazy fart smellers want to turn back the clock. Spend less on today's America than we did in 1928? How the hell does that make any sense? Ignore the last 85 years? Let's go back to the good old days of the Gilded Age. That's crazy. Pitiful thinking, just pitiful.

But wait a minute. The Gilded Age, that has a nice ring to it; the Gilded Age was a time of peace and prosperity. Hell, just read *The Great Gatsby* if you don't believe me.

Here's the rub. The Gilded Age was a time of great prosperity for some. Much like the 1980s and 90s and today, it was a time when the wealthy were *exceedingly* wealthy, but most folks were just getting by. Read anything by William Faulkner, or Jack London, or Theodore Dreiser, or Langston Hughes, or Erskine Caldwell, if you don't believe me. And the Gilded Age was anything but peaceful. In the decades leading up to the Great Depression, labor unions and companies (and their hired goons) were routinely clashing violently in the streets, hundreds of thousands killed or maimed—ever hear of the Ludlow Massacre? The little guy was fighting for his share of the pie. A time of peace and prosperity? Only if you rewrite history.

We all paid a pretty heavy price for the Gilded Age, in the form of the Great Depression. Do Republicans really want to go back to the Gilded Age? Yes, they certainly do. It was a hell of a good time for the very rich, and that's what your GOP is all about these days. One look at the last Republican presidential candidate, Mitt Romney, pretty much tells you all you need to know about the GOP of today.

If a return to the Gilded Age sounds like a revolutionary idea, that's because it is. Crazy as this sounds, the Republican Party has become a party of revolution backwards, rather than evolution.

Republicans have come to be known as the Party that Favors Revolution, to distinguish themselves from the Party that favors Evolution.

You see, Democrats—liberals or conservatives, you know what I mean—believe in legislation keeping pace with the activity of man in discovery, in invention, and in the manipulation of accumulated wealth (to paraphrase Sir Henry Maine). Now, the conflict between today's Republicans and Democrats is not about discovery, invention, manipulation or accumulated wealth. Both favor those goodies. It's about the word "pace." Democrats believe in legislation keeping up with them zingers. They think of themselves as the party evolving toward solutions in a timely manner. Not to a hip-hop or boogie beat; more like a Glenn Miller "In the Mood" rhythm.

By contrast, Republicans sing "pace" to the tune of "Rock of Ages." Their great apprehension is unintended consequences, which they believe Democrats overlook or minimize. There is merit to this worry; there's not a piece of legislation that doesn't harbor unintended consequences. There's a lesson from the Shadow here. You know his slogan: "who knows what evil lurks in the hearts of men? The Shadow knows." Well, today's "conservatives" see the lurking evil in the interlines of the Constitution.

Who knows what evil lurks in the hearts of legislation? Republicans know (or claim they do): unintended consequences. It may take a decade, even half a century for the damn things to surface, but they will. Oh, yes, they will. And what was the terrible unintended consequence of FDR's New Deal? A bunch of spoiled, lazy, mooching Americans, sucking life from the government teat.

Horseshit.

But this so-called "rule of unintended consequences" is why Republicans define "pace" to mean "no," "not yet," "someday," "not 'til the 11th hour," and shout "the sky is falling" and "resist until the mob is about to revolt." Better the unintended consequences of revolution than the unintended consequences of legislation that leads to child labor laws and equal pay for women. Damn it, think of the unintended consequences!

We're the party of revolution, see. Not until the cusp of revolution do we legislate. That's how we buy time to ferret out the unintended consequences of discovery, invention, and the manipulation of accumulated wealth, to say nothing of ferreting out the consequences of legislating on behalf of clean air and water or the rights of Tiny Tim, Huckleberry Finn, Forest Gump or Trayvon Martin. It's our theory of government, see. Stability achieved through revolutionary change rather than evolutionary change. You know, like the Civil War, or the Great Depression, or the Civil Rights Movement of the 60s. Just wait until the wound festers.

Problem is, circumspection in legislation is a legitimate theory of government, but like all theories of government when hesitancy is carried obsessively to extremes, two things happen. First, government becomes dysfunctional. Second, the mob takes over and substitutes sloganeering for thought and power for governing.

Hence, Benghazi displaces thinking about how to go about things differently; and starve the poor in order to get them off their duffs to look for work replaces thoughtful legislation that funds updating the nation's highways and bridges and waterways and thus creates hundreds of thousands of jobs for lots of different people.

Duh!

RANT #8

Can Democrats Survive Democracy?

My fellow conservatives, what was once unthinkable has become a no-brainer: our party has been taken over by loons and it's time either to take the party back or vote Democrat—the real conservatives these days.

As much as I hate to say it, I feel that the only way to really clean our own house up is to vote Democratic in 2014 and 2016. I'm not suggesting anyone change their voter registration in order to vote in primaries. Remain GOP republicans (with a little r), but return the Grand to the party. Do the Texas Two-Step, vote Democratic until the party puts in place leaders who want to govern rather than rule.

Is there another choice? I'm afraid I don't see one, for reasons discussed below.

Here is what's at stake: can democracy survive democracy?

Answering that question is the great test confronting emerging generations. Consider it this way. For a moment let's concentrate on the meaning of the term "mob" as the Founding Fathers thought of it. "Mob" to them meant people who didn't own property. It helps to recognize what it didn't mean to them. It didn't mean fuzzy-minded sons-of-guns claiming each was an island, sovereign and immune from government. And "mob" didn't mean rude people who didn't own property and had nothing to do but rabble-rouse. No, "mob" to the Founding Fathers meant people who didn't have a property stake in government. The notion was that if a person didn't own land, real property, a business or suchlike, he couldn't be considered a stakeholder in a society of Contract (that is, a society that valued merit and ability over class or status). There had to be some measure of worth other than character. Religion was one, property another. Delaware at one time required ownership of 50 acres or the possession 40 English pounds to vote. Either was a hunk in 1800, but enough to let you vote without the propertied-class having to fear your lack of allegiance to that class. As John Adams put his apprehensions, "everyman who had not a farthing, will demand an equal voice with any other"—meaning himself, of course.

Turns out the Founding Fathers grossly misjudged the character of the property-less classes. Once given the chance to have a say in things, the still property-less, but now eligible voter (and thus stakeholder in society) proved to be cautious and circumspect. Over 200 years of voting in ever larger numbers they've revealed their disposition to be not only conservative and pragmatic, but also more conservative and pragmatic than the propertied-classes in many cases.

Catch your breath for a moment. The greatest successful experiment of American democracy has been the admission of non-property owning citizens into the voter's booth. There can be little doubt that it's a stabilizing force. Historically speaking, it's a quantum leap in human progression.

So, what's this "can democracy survive democracy" business?

Well, to say it more precisely: can democracy survive the democratization of money? When the Republican appointed majority on the Supreme Court held that corporations were persons wearing masks, and that there can be no limit placed on the amount of money individuals and "persons wearing masks" can contribute to political candidates, it essentially took us from "one man one vote" to "one dollar one vote." Obviously, Rupert Murdock can contribute many times more money to a candidate than you or I can. And if you don't believe that this means he has many times more influence than you or I do, then you might as well stop reading now. You've got water on the brain. The fat cats have gobbled up most of the real influence, and it isn't hard to understand why so many Americans are so jaded about politics—they feel, not unfairly, that representative government doesn't really mean anything anymore.

In fact, the opposite is true. The proof is in the propaganda. Ask yourself why the fat cats are spending so much time and energy and money to get *you* to see things the way they do? If *your* vote didn't matter, why would they do that? The very existence of the wool being pulled over your eyes, the smoke-and-mirrors show being put on for you, is the first and best clue to the power you hold in your hands, dear voter.

The challenge for ordinary conservatives is how to vote in candidates who are forthright about themselves, do not use financial magic to mislead, want to govern rather than rule, and who understand that the greatest foundational sentiment for a conservative is to broaden the circle of those we include.

First is to learn to smell fish. If something smells fishy, it's probably a fish. That fishy smell is your first clue to the wool and the smoke-and-mirrors.

Second, we honest ordinary conservatives need to recognize that the rich, and especially the super-rich, do not share with us the same values and interests. The rich, and again especially the super-rich, are creating islands within our country, well-insulated and hermetically sealed enclaves, where they are safe from, and oblivious to, the increasing squalor and degradation of American society. Their lives—and livelihoods—are well secured. They're not worried about losing a job; they're not worried about an expensive illness that might cost them their home; they're not worried about sending their kids to a good college; they're certainly not worried about the car breaking down or the rent being overdue.

But most of us are worried about one or two or

all of the above, aren't we? Does anybody believe that Mitt Romney shares those worries with you? Or John Boehner? Or Mitch McConnell? Not hardly.

So, to that fishy smell. Follow the money, as any good detective will tell you. The trick is to find out *who* is supporting which candidate. Here's a good rule of thumb: if a billionaire is backing a candidate, it's a safe bet that candidate isn't too interested in *your* concerns. (Of course we've all heard of limousine liberals, but those folks are mostly *millionaires*, not *billionaires*—big difference if you do the math). So, if you find that the Koch brothers, for example, are supporting a certain candidate, a vote for that candidate is a vote for Koch interests, not your own.

The radicalized Supreme Court has delivered us a big piece of trouble here. In the same ruling that made corporations into people, the court held that those donations to Political Action Committees (PACs) in support of one candidate or another can be *kept anonymous*. This, of course, makes it difficult to find out who is supporting who. You beginning to recognize that fishy smell yet?

RANT #9

The Shadow of
Unintended Consequences

Somewhere in my 80-year journey toward a semblance of wisdom I learned a key lesson. If you want to win friends and influence people, disarm their fears at the get go.

Not only will they share their private agenda, but they'll listen. Observe animal behavior. Some dogs, for example, approach a meeting wagging their tails, others showing their teeth; either way they make a threat assessment. "First impression" is how we'd put it today. Disarming fears, wagging your tail, works with students, ordinary sorts, honchos in business, and even politicians.

What fear or threat motivates today's Republicans? I could answer that with a line from Elizabeth Barrett Browning, "let me count the ways," but that would be snide. I won't do that. Instead, I'll just discuss one fear that tells us a lot about the real agenda.

From the merely-rich to the uber-rich, they fear

education. Not technical education, like engineering or mathematics or business administration, but liberal education (and not just because it's called *liberal*). A few of the Social Sciences, like anthropology and maybe history, may be okay if taught the right way; but sociology, psychology, philosophy and any political science that deals with people getting along horizontally rather than vertically is verboten. Dangerous stuff.

Those inclined toward Mammon fear the Humanities most. Art, drama and literature may be amusing sometimes, but they can be disruptive. Take *My Fair Lady* for instance—women's rights disguised in tunes and opulent staging. Or Upton Sinclair's, *The Jungle*, which raised public awareness and an outcry and forced safety standards and labor fairness in the meat-packing industry. Or Victor Hugo's, *Les Miserables*, which alerted the whole world to the unfair travails of the poor and disadvantaged. Or Dickins' *Oliver Twist*, which did much the same.

The Humanities promote wild and evil ideas, like looking at things abstractly, holistically, to say nothing of critically and comparatively. Think of Huck Finn. It's dangerous when the little guys like Huck start thinking for themselves; he might get the idea that the current arrangement of society isn't quite what it should be, or could be; he gets crazy ideas like justice and fairness and *rights*.

In other words, subjects like ethics, moral philosophy, religion or political theory that treat with the ideal or best-possible-world are seedbeds of unintended consequences. That is why funding endowments and chairs for Mammon-economics (trickle-down BS) departments are a fad today among millionaires and billionaires. Education today means bottom-line profits for the corporate culture. Disciplines that promote profit of the soul don't deserve funding. Education should be job-training, not life-training. Let small university presses wither and Humanities departments gasp for funding, while profit-generating fields like engineering and science and business drown in cash. Profit over people.

It all makes perfect sense, for robots. If life is short, nasty and brutish, doesn't it follow that the only worthy philosophy is a philosophy of resignation and acceptance? In his book, *You Can't Go Home Again*, a young Thomas Wolfe rejected a Philosophy of Acceptance and advocated a Philosophy of Found. In the heat of the Great Depression, he wrote, "I believe that we are lost here in America but I believe we shall be found…and this is our dream to be accomplished."

". . . to be *accomplished*." This is a preamble to the Great Society. In these two paragraphs Wolfe captures the conflict between how Republicans feel about unintended consequences and how Democrats do. Both accept that there have been and always will be such. But one approaches the future like a man protecting himself by holding his hand before him proceeding into a dark room unknown to him, and the other like a scout on a hill shading his eyes from the sun so he can look into the distance.

I think of Wolfe as the Founder of a Found

Generation, as opposed to the Lost Generation caused by the Great Depression. He had faith in America's economic potential, but a greater faith in America as a holistic abstraction blessed with the "glorious assurance" of a dream to be accomplished. Isn't that what the Preamble to the Constitution of the United States is? A dream to be accomplished? I think so.

Another insight from Wolfe. "Man is born to be eternally beset and preyed upon by all of the monsters of his own creation," describes how some Republicans view FDR's New Deal. Follow their line of reasoning and the unintended consequence of that monster of human creation begat the Great Society, which begat Big Government. Horror of horrors!

Begats begat unintended consequences, no question there. Yet the Great Society was not the unintended consequence of the New Deal. It was the *intended* consequence, the "true discovery of America . . . our mighty and immortal land yet to come . . . the true discovery of our own democracy." That was the intent of the New Deal/Great Society. Yet conservatives are correct: both led to unintended consequences of a culture by dependence. Like wealthy people demanding tax breaks and loopholes in the tax code as if they were newly-hatched birds jostling for food from their mother's beak. Like rich corporations craving subsidies. Like big farmer gobbling up the bulk of federal welfare instead of small farmer. Like too-big-to-fail banks exacting subsidies to cover their asses after taking slot-machine risks. Like states refusing to tax their citizens enough to build highways, recover from tornadoes, feed or educate their babes, or help Tiny Tim, Forest Gump or the autistic.

Upward dependence is what it's called; and all the while mocking the dependence of the truly downtrodden. The choice is clear: upward dependence or downward. Upward dependence is a hell-bent race to the bottom, is what it is. Which party will take us into the future?

I empathize with conservatives and their worry about the monstrous creations of man. Let's take a peek at another good idea that has taken the unintended consequences route.

It begins with Sir Henry Maine's 1861 observation that the pace of "discovery, invention and the manipulation of accumulated wealth" had exceeded the ability of legislators to keep up. He was spot on. Forty-seven years later, in 1908, Harvard University realized that was true not just of legislators, but also—hold your hats—of all people—businessmen. And so they launched the Harvard School of Business—all kinds of unintended consequences come straight from there.

The Industrial Revolution, beginning let's say 1750, begat a Society of Contract like you wouldn't believe. In Contract, according to Sir Henry, borrowing money from family and kin gave way to borrowing money from strangers, and contracting or investing with strangers, and becoming wealthy without working. (Working here means farmers, coal miners, roofers, washer-women, shop owners, i.e.

the bulk of humanity.)

It was a fantastic idea. Wizard of Oz financing begat business, businesses begat corporations, corporations begat bigger corporations, which begat conglomerates, which begat cartels, which begat monopolies, which . . . well, you can see how this "monstrous creation of man" got out of hand.

That's not quite the whole story. There were observers of Mammon-in-heat who realized that huge sums of money were being left on the table by unprofessional businessmen who did not know how to run a business. Enter Harvard School of Business, the how-to-do-it-business-school of the future and *prima donna* of the emerging secular culture.

You could search academic papers going back to Plato and find no more chaste an idea than the Harvard Business School. Created in 1908, its purpose was as virginal as a virgin idea can be: a school for diplomacy and government service offering a degree in the humanities field, with a major in business. However, keeping up with discovery, invention and wealth manipulation, soon led to non-humanities courses in Government, Accounting, Business, Finance, Management, Marketing, Negotiation, Strategy, Technology, Organizational Behavior, Operations Management, and more.

Long story short, somewhere, date undetermined, the major in business gobbled up the degree in humanities, trumped the study of the best and ideal that men and societies could be. Soon graduates skilled in how to make a buck professionally in the short term figured out how wealth could become greater wealth with a little bit of . . . manipulation, and soon Harvard's Hasty Pudding Club had a rival—the Hasty Profits Club. You know those credit-default-swaps and collateralized-debt-obligations you've heard about? Yeah, thank the Harvard MBAs and others for those little pieces of financial dynamite. Thank these near-sighted hot-shots for our modern form of Casino Capitalism. What on earth would we do without traders who make $4 billion a year while selling America to the dogs?

In less than 100 years Sir Henry's observation of 1861 was writ large in America in the 20th Century, but that's far from the end of the story. There's more: wealth manipulation begat the lobbyist— political manipulation. And the lobbyist begat the fund-me-legislator, who threw his lot in with the lobbyists and manipulators and they strangled the regulations, opened up the Wall Street Casino, and begat the financial crash of 2007-08, and begat the economic depression that followed, and begat the slow strangling of the middle class. Thanks fellas.

That's one lesson of unintended consequences: once you start the begatting it's hard to stop it— because you'd have to admit that you were wrong. And you can't do that. Oh no . . . it's a recipe for calamity.

So much for begatting. But wait, there's more. The economic crash begat a citizenry struggling seven years later, and begat a growing wealth and income gap that looks a lot like the days when slaves built pyramids for pharaohs, or the Gilded Age, for that matter. Now the guy or gal earning $35,000 a year has to wonder if they're anything more than slaves.

And with galling hypocrisy "conservatives" snicker "I told you so." As in: life is short, nasty and brutish; doom is inherent and inevitable in the "monstrous creations of man." Even when we follow our best intentions the perverse is inevitable. See, I told you so. Even good intentions like Harvard 1908 turn out to have a bad side.

Keep the faith, dear reader. All is not lost. At Columbia Business School as of 2009, an ethics course is required; that's "an," as in one course. At Wharton as of 2009, seven professors teach an assortment of ethics classes. That's how much ground the Ten Commandments have lost to Mammon. But all is not lost at Harvard either; in 2009, about 160 graduates signed "the MBA Oath," a pledge to refrain from advancing their own ambitions at the expense of the humanities—others or society. That's the good news; the bad news is that 640 graduates did *not* sign it.

Although this "MBA Oath" has spread worldwide, many CEOs in 2014 think the oath is naïve. Where's the short-term profit, they snicker. They seem to believe that greed is good economics and results in stable government.

Fear not. We can't expect too much too soon; that's not how most unintended consequences play out. It takes a while for ethics to trickle up into corporate governance. The day is long before it could become commonplace for a CEO to choose the interest of the workers or the community over an increase in profit. That day is still lost in space.

It's likely to stay lost too, at least as long as this Mammon notion rules: the dividend for one share of stock is more valuable than one person's vote. Let me repeat that: stock more valuable than citizenship? Oh yes, in the corporate age of Mammon the dividend is more important than a vote. When future historians write about our Republic they will likely portray the Rubicon that distinguishes its decline from its fall as the decades when money replaced citizenship as the purpose of America. Or, put differently, when the Supreme Court elevated corporate personhood over citizenship personhood. Or, put differently again, when one dollar superseded one vote.

Republicans are ruled by fear—fear of unintended consequences. Unless, of course, Mammon is on their side. To hell with the consequences if there's money to be made. Of course.

RANT #10

Tea Party Astroturf

What were original Tea Partiers mad at? Not Obama. Bush. The Bush who was too chicken to pay for two ill-thought-out wars that dragged on and on and ran up huge deficits. The Bush who one-upped the Democrats by launching a new social program—prescription medicines—without paying for it and running up the deficit ever more. The Bush who didn't initially deregulate Wall Street—that had been done before—but deregulated it more and turned his back on the problems that exploded into the Great Recession. The Bush who ended his presidency by bailing out "Too Big to Fail" capitalists, adding almost another trillion to the national debt (for openers).

To my knowledge no president has accumulated more debt in more ways in less time than President George W. Bush. No wonder conservatives, either Democrat or Republican, and Independents went ballistic. Bush came across as a circus barker for a lousy economic show who turned tail when the worst got worse. He had talked as if he were a conservative, but walked like someone drunk on Everyman's money. Bailing out Wall Street was the straw that broke the backs not only of prudent Republicans, but also prudent Democrats and Independents. It was Bush directly, and Obama only indirectly, that those who felt Bush had ambushed them were angry at. The Original Tea Partiers had cause to be angry; the Loudmouths who took over the movement are merely demigods disguised as Original Tea Partiers. It's worth asking: is their artful disguise one reason the CCC adores them? (Caucasians Camouflaged as Christians.)

Original Tea Partiers want reform; want a return to *tax citizenship*. They're the empty sleeves of today. Loudmouth Tea Partiers seek power. They personify egocentrism as a cultural value.

It must be asked, where did the Original Tea Partiers go wrong? Here's one of my colleagues' viewpoint: It's completely silly to call the Tea Party movement "grassroots." At best, it's Astroturf. The wing-nut goons of big-business and big-wealth that conjured the schizophrenic movement up out of thin air have mastered the rhetoric of populism, but the aims and intentions of Tea Partyism are entirely aristocratic and plutocratic—and entirely undemocratic, un-American.

It's important to remember that one-third of the passengers on the *Mayflower* were not Puritans, but "boarders" who filled empty slots; and by paying their own way they made the voyage financially possible. Without the secularist's money, the *Mayflower* and its hyper-religious mission would likely never have sailed. Some secularists signed the "Mayflower Compact," some didn't. These secular travelers were interested in establishing themselves economically in the New World and had little if any interest in religion.

It's also important to remember that about a third of the New World colonists did not want to rebel against Great Britain. Known as Tory's, they opposed the independence movement. For the most part, these Tory's were wealthy landowners, but mainly of the merchant class who had lucrative financial and trade relationships with the Mother Country. They feared that revolution would break these relationships, cut off their sources of wealth and leave them with a diminished lifestyle. How fervently they fought against revolution is a story from American history that hasn't been sufficiently told. It's a story of vested interests standing in the way of progress, and that is just about exactly what today's Tea Party is doing. The American Revolution does represent progress, doesn't it?

After the War of Independence, the Brits could have dumped the colonies and left them to survive as a pauper nation eating maize. But the King *et al* needed the colonial trade as much as the newly independent nation did. The "Tory" trade relationship not only survived, but thrived; it is often overlooked as a reason why the United States got off to a decent economic start; the Founding Fathers never cut themselves off from the mother teat. The revolution and its unintended consequences turned out to be good for northern aristocrats, southern planters, and Everyman, too (except the slave). This is one of the foundational principles of Democratic Capitalism: all benefit; "all" as in ALL; ALL— including the "empty sleeves" Jefferson Davis advised the troops and the young ladies to choose.

Lincoln fully recognized this, as reflected in his policy of conciliation, amnesty, and affirmative action toward the post-war south (covered in Rant #3), clearly values repudiated by the Loudmouth Tea Partiers.

It's repetitive, but important to recall who the rank-and-file were originally mad at. It was George W. Bush. This was for several reasons that I've briefly touched on above. First, he launched a new Big Government program to provide prescription drug benefits to the citizenry at large. Second, he didn't fund that program, which caused the deficit to escalate. Third, he launched a merited war against the Taliban in Afghanistan, also without funding it, adding to the deficit. Fourth, he launched an unmerited war in Iraq without funding it, increasing the deficit by trillions and counting. Then to cap off this credit-card orgy, he launched another Big Government program, the TARP bail out, when the economy turned upside down in 2007-08. He didn't budget-fund any of it. It was all done by what is called "off budget," which means it's hidden so the media won't rub it in your noses.

Big government programs, big government deficits, big government wars poorly managed resulting in more big government deficits; big recession with more deficits; huge bail out with no accountability. "Enough already!" shouted the original Tea Partiers.

The Bush Administration took the economy to the brink of the abyss. In particular, it took the middle class to the cleaners by sucking trillions of dollars out of their collective pockets. This was government neither by naiveté nor by innocence, but by reckless self-interest. Nine-year-olds who are that out of control with money were taken to the woodshed during the era that the Republican philosophers admire so much. It should be no surprise to the GOP gurus that that's exactly what everyman Republican, Democrat and Independent wanted to do. They came out of the woodwork, protested, created the Tea Party, and in the disorientation that accompanies anger voted *tax citizenship* legislators out of office, replaced them with *tax Norquistism* con-men, and blamed Obama for the whole mess. The new president was an innocent victim, but anger causes people to misidentify the enemy.

Most if not all Original Tea Partiers are good, fair-minded folks (Dagnabbit, I have to say that; I was one of them, though closeted). While original populist anger at Bush was fully justified, their anger at Obama represents a mistaken transference of blame; he was the quarterback called to step in place of the failed predecessor. In street terms, Bush sowed, Obama reaped.

There is another side to the story. Those websites and organizations that organized and built the protest movement were anything but populist in agenda (it's a safe bet that the Koch brothers had a hand in funding them). Imagine a populist movement fighting for tax cuts for the richest among us? Imagine a populist movement fighting for the right of employers to exploit their employees? Imagine a populist movement fighting *against* voting-rights? Imagine a populist movement attempting to destroy the social safety-net? There's nothing populist—nor popular—about any of this.

The Original rank-and-file Tea Partier has been played for a fool by egocentric demagogues sensing a chance at power with no real philosophy of government but tax avoidance for the better off. Unwittingly he's become a stooge, a dupe. Answer this question: Who wants lower taxes, less regulations and smaller government more: Big Money or Everyman? Planter aristocrat or Empty Sleeve? Tea Partiers have been played for the dummy of Big Money's ventriloquist, mouthing his talking points and coded blabber about thee comes after ME (if at all).

So, the Tea Party movement is a conspiracy? No, it's just more Kabuki theater, more wool over average American eyes.

I'll discuss this more in Volume 2, but some Republican philosophers see enormous deficits as a way to dismember the New Deal and lynch liberal thinking. "Bring on *tax Norquistism* and its resulting big deficits," they screamed at Bush 43, mouthing the Reagan mantra. It became one part of a three-part ideological strategy: (a) increase deficits while simultaneously cutting the throat of any new taxes and bleeding revenues wherever possible; (b) all the while gutting Great Society programs for lower and middle class welfare; and (c) drive a stake through liberalisms heart from which it will never rise from the grave to haunt anti-Lincoln Republicans. Lambs marked for slaughter have a better chance at survival. The importance of this three-pronged game plan can't be underestimated. It is a stranglehold on any attempt by Democrats or Republicans alike to provide for the constitutionally mandated General Welfare or Domestic Tranquility. Death to the New Deal. Death to the Great Society. Death to liberalism and its alleged intent to control you. Today's Tea Party demagogic movement is serving this ideology very well. Enter the 1,000 year Reich of the non-Lincoln Republican Party. No more government of, by and for the people.

This dreamed-of and sought-after death of "liberalism" did not mean the end of corporate liberalism. Oh no. The philosophers heralded crony corporate welfare as the essential and compelling meaning of "general welfare" (more of this trickle-down gibberish, of course). As a substitute for "liberalism," the philosophers and practitioners replaced the imprudent government of Bush with "corporatism" (corporations are now people, remember). In the ruckus about deficits, the anger of the rank-and-file Tea Partiers has been used to the benefit of corporate "people" and the very rich. It's a classic bait-and-switch. What the rank-and-file Tea Partiers want is good government; what the "official" Tea Party wants is no government interference with industry, but plenty of government money *for* industry. When you, Mr. and Ms. Everyman, shout out for smaller government and fewer regulations and less taxation, you're mouthing what Big Money wants; they have conned you into thinking it's what you want. They're using you, Mr. and Ms. Everyman. They're using you. The more you do their propaganda work for them the more Big Corporations sit back and rub their fat bellies in glee.

No one wants smaller government, fewer regulations and lower taxes more than the corporations do. Don't for a moment think that everyman on the street wants these things more than corporations do. The desire, demand and propaganda for it come straight from the top down. "Corporatism" co-opted and twisted the values and ideals that rank-and-file Tea Partiers are shouting for.

These ideas—"corporatism," death to the New Deal, etc.—are nothing new, of course. They have been the core of the right-wing of the Republican Party for 40 years—and they are *not* conservative, as I've tried to show. What the Tea Party movement represents is a doubling-down on these wrong-headed philosophies of government; it represents the drift of fringe ideas toward the center of Republicanism. Rarely before has the average, genuinely conservative everyman Republican been reduced to a pawn in the game of politics for power as blatantly and unashamedly as today. "Tea Partier" is now synonymous with "loudmouth idiot," but the ideological damage has been done—and continues, somehow, to be done. It's a train-wreck for the honest conservative, and it's another step down in the decline of the Republican brand.

As the corporatist ideologues and other loudmouths usurped the genuine Tea Party movement the populist anger only grew more furious. But where to turn? By 2008 the fury was directed at Bush, and rightly so. Enter fate, lucky Bush left the White House just in time, with his tail between his legs; and unlucky Obama entered the presidency with the bulls-eye squarely on his back. Obama took the helm just as the nation entered economic free-fall.

Psychologists call it transference.

Wool and political Kabuki Theater have managed to make Obama the scapegoat, in the eyes of many. And the loudmouth Tea Party has been a big help. Hide Bush; Blame Obama! The more he can be made to look like the fool from Kenya, the more Bushwreck is forgotten. Republican philosophers and practitioners have done everything possible to camouflage Bush/Republican responsibility for the financial crisis and the economic collapse, while heaping blame on the black man in the White House. It's worse than politics as blood-sport; it's politics without a theory of governing, and it's killing America.

Recovering Tea Partiers never want to see another George W. Bush, and Ted Cruz has made "Never another pretend conservative like Bush. All we want is a pure conservative." his theme song. Yet the posturing demigod Cruz is badly misreading what even many loudmouth Tea Partiers want: they want *good* government, not *no* government. Your average Tea Partier *wants* his Social Security checks, his Medicare assistance, his unemployment insurance. Cruz wants to destroy these things.

What future does the honest conservative—and yes, populist—have? First of all, we have to take back our slogans and reassert efficient government and lower deficits as synonyms for good government. It's a delicate task. Ne'er-do-wells will always gravitate toward blood-sport sloganeering, but anger and hate are not what good conservatives are about. Second, we must avoid being the sloganeering mouthpiece of crony corporate capitalism; this means we need to seize the populist anger and become the party willing to check corporate malfeasance—yes, with regulation (that dirty word!)—and we need to become the party of fair taxation, which, yes, means a progressive tax whereby the rich and corporations pay in proportion to their means. That is true fiscal conservatism, and its methods and aims are biblical.

RANT #11

Volume 2 and Full Disclosure

Volume 2 will include Rants about the Supreme Court, Jefferson Davis and the Confederacy, more about the party of Lincoln and the anti-Lincoln party and who knows what else.

Here, however, in the name of full disclosure, let me recount my political family tree. I have voted Republican and Democrat in national, state and local elections throughout my voting life, but have considered myself an Independent for the past 40 years or so. In Florida I am a registered Democrat because Independents don't get to participate in primary elections, and the current Republican Party scares me.

My Quaker grandmother was the first political influence in my life. She was my babysitter as an infant and taught me through the slats of my crib to say God and Jesus before I said Da-da or Ma-ma. As an adult I have several times reexamined her tutorials and remain convinced that our Judeo-Christian heritage is one of the greatest developments in world history.

Mother Nature was the second political influence in my life. From birth to six I spent most of my time at the foot of Long's Peak outside Rocky Mountain National Park near Estes Park, Colorado. My paternal grandfather owned a camp for boys there, and Gray Wolf, a Sioux elder, was my caregiver. He taught me to walk through the forest without making a sound, to listen to Aspen trees clipping a hymn of the wonders of Mother Nature, and we smoked the peace-pipe, so to speak, while I sat in his lap watching the sunset.

The third person to influence me politically was a man I call the Admiral—a man my mother took up with. I admit to a love-hate relationship with him. Hate because after my nuclear family imploded, he filled the vacuum with venom. My mother moved in with him in sin to raise his two children while abandoning my sister and me to separate foster homes. She sold us out for money, and that crime is hers, but the Admiral directed that chorus of events. One of his orchestrations was the number he did on my young, curious, happy, healthy self-image; his double-edged tongue could whittle a person's thinking about himself into a pile of shavings in 20 seconds flat. At the age of seven he precipitated an identity crisis in me; at least that's what my first psychiatrist said, and I tend to feel that's true. It all but bankrupted me mentally until I had a little help from my friends.

At the age of seven the Admiral sent me to foster home number one, and for that I'm grateful. The year was 1940 and the Colorado Military

Academy was a wonderful place for a second-grader to be. The clouds of war were shadowing out all else important in life, and I was there among other cadets listening to the reports about Pearl Harbor. I have vivid memories of being selected for the revelry team that raised the flag in that cold winter, our boots crunching the frost at dawn as we marched around the parade grounds. I shared with the Admiral my decision to become a General in the U.S. Army, but he quickly poo-pooed that idea and told me I'd never make it as a grunt private let alone a swab in the Navy.

I learned to speak three languages at the Academy: the language of the soldier, that of the gentleman, and then, of course, how to talk dirty. I never took up acting dirty—too much left in me of the Quaker from my days in the crib, I guess.

What was there to love about the Admiral? He was as patriotic as a person could be and devoted to becoming president of the Sons of the American Revolution. He was anti-communist to the hilt, a John Bircher before there was a John Birch Society, and he was Republican through and through. Ages eight and nine, I, too, was Republican through and through.

The fourth political influence in my life occurred the next year. I mutinied after one of the Admiral's tongue-lashings and he sent me into exile. I was ten and in foster home number two, a private family living on the prairie of eastern Colorado near the Nebraska border. Harsh country in winter, full of hard working people. There I eavesdropped on farmers who had it all during the 1920s, but had nothing after the Great Depression; they were beholden to Franklin Delano Roosevelt's New Deal for saving not just their skins, but their way of life, too. If there ever was a synonym for Hallelujah or Amen in politics, it was FDR for these folks and their families.

The fifth political influence in my life came in foster home number three, about a year later. Another private family, this one living in the foothills west of Denver. Middle age, they never had children; still the experiment went fairly well for the three of us. The year was 1943-44 and night after night I sat at their feet while we listened to the radio, and Edward R. Murrow's reports of the war's progress. Lem had a club foot, and could never serve in the military, but he was a grateful citizen and I would have to use all 20 fingers and toes to count the ways of his gratitude. He bought me huge maps of the two war theaters and after every broadcast together we'd move the pins of progress (and sometimes setback) as we followed the course of the war against evil. Lem was a salesman for New York Life Insurance and that represented the Republican side of him. The Democratic side of him was reflected in my nickname for him—Gideon— because he was active in the bible distribution campaign of the Gideon movement and would give the coat he wore to someone who needed it. It's not possible, is it, for an 11-year-old castaway to forget carrying bibles for the lame man as he delivered them to hotels and those new things called motels?

Lem was, in hindsight, my role model in becoming politically independent.

These were formative experiences, and I believe they have a lot to do with my eventual political makeup.

I cast my first presidential vote in 1952, for Eisenhower, and again for him in 1956. I voted for Kennedy in 1960—but that was as much a vote against Nixon as it was for Kennedy. Lyndon Johnson's stance on Civil Rights and for what the Great Society represented earned him my vote in 1964, but it was that year also that I began to drift dramatically away from the new Republican Party.

That was a watershed election, two or three notches more significant than the usual. Where most presidential elections represent a choice between personalities and policies, the 1964 election represented a clash of philosophies within the Republican Party. On the one hand was the Eastern or Progressive Republican Party that, the way I saw it, was heir to Lincoln's ideals. On the other hand was the emerging Republican brand that could be heard to say something like: "I don't like what America is becoming; us old white folks need to take back our country and return things to the way they were in good ol' yesteryear." There's a hint of hysteria to the latter; a suggestion of protest against progress; and a bit more than a hint of racism and xenophobia.

That protest had been brewing for years, but the 1964 election brought the split within the Republican Party into the open. It has festered ever since, and the pus of disagreement and ideological confusion has infected not just the Party, but also, now, Congress' ability to govern the body politic. It has meant that the Republican Party has become a party longing for a mythical past, and thus has been forced to adopt one defensive strategy after another. At the heart of this philosophical decline is the worship of Mammon (the Golden Calf in Biblical terms), and the notion America is about Mammon, and little else, the Ten Commandments just camouflage. This is the seedbed where the perverse justifications for income instability and the political instability it promotes have grown from.

It's avarice, this worship of the Golden Calf. In today's Republican-speak, it's American as it should be, but it is an insult to the Ten Commandments, our national heritage, and Judeo-Christian teachings. It is unworthy of our conservative ideals.

I feel a word about my stance in the classroom is warranted. As an undergraduate at Lafayette College (a third engineering student, a third business administration, a third liberal arts) I was introduced to interdisciplinary living, one of the greatest teachers I have had in life. I majored in history with a minor in government, but the education I had was in the humanities and civics, not politics. That distinction may not mean much today, but civics is the study of *ideal* government, the best government, the just society, as well as the workings of everyday politics. Civics and humanities, are value-oriented courses of study; they hold people and societies accountable for their behavior. They admit to a kernel of truth in Edmund Burke's "life is short, nasty and brutish." But they also admit the full acorn of truth in Socrates' admonition to "know thyself," and its implication that "know thyself" applies to societies as well as individuals. FDR's New Deal and Lyndon Johnson's Great Society were attempts at just that—attempts to know our society and hence to see our weaknesses, and thus correct those flaws. Civics and the humanities, in other words, help us ask the right questions.

My Masters at the University of Pennsylvania was in International Relations, or more broadly, the study of good and functional government on a global scale. My Doctorate at the University of Colorado was in Political Theory and Constitutional Law under Clark Bouton and Richard Wilson, the former a professor of civics if there ever was one, and the latter a professor deeply concerned with how to apply the lessons of civics to everyday cases of political disputes. Theory and practice, vision and application, have been leitmotivs of my formal education. Each of the three institutions presented me with the opportunity America is famous for, the opportunity to change my mind for the better. I had the opportunity to further expand my thinking via interdisciplinary studies, first as a teaching assistant at the University of Colorado, and later as a professor at St. Andrews Presbyterian College. Team Teaching with chemists, biologists, psychologists, economists, religion, history, philosophy, theater and other professors forces the mind to expand, I can assure you.

As a college professor myself I tried to apply those leitmotivs in the classroom. It didn't matter if it was Republican better or Democrat better. I used business cards with the imprint of an elephant on one corner and a donkey on the other, a reflection of my attempt to be Independent in the classroom and community. No student would accuse me of being a flaming Republican, nor a flaming Democrat. Passionate about civics, yes, but avoiding the imprint of ideology.

I regarded each student as a granule in a cold-release time-capsule—one designed to seek his or her potential today, others tomorrow or the day after. My role was never to indoctrinate; my job in the classroom was to help each student learn to ask the questions they needed to in order to form their own political orbit.

I chose to teach at a college that was as barrier-free as I could find. About 10% of the students were handicapped in some physical way (many Vietnam vets, lupus or muscular dystrophy sufferers, etc.). Three of my pre-law "wheelies"—a term of endearment, I assure you—went on to law schools, including one to Duke University. I'm quite proud of all. Good People, 150 years ago my wheelies would have died near birth, or been hidden in the basements or attics of social disapproval, like Boo in *To Kill a Mockingbird.* It has been a privilege, an honor and a responsibility to live at a time of new horizons.

You can see why I cringe at what the anti-Lincoln party is doing to America's potential. At the end of the congressional year, when you can read summaries of how this or that representative voted, and you see that some voted against funding for autistic children or the handicapped, or voted against pay decent enough to attract and keep outstanding teachers in public schools; when you look at these voting records through the civics microscope, you wonder "What in hell are they thinking? What planet do they live on? What do they think today's Americans are? What kind of nation do they want for future generations? Are these the people I want representing me?"

There are more Rants to come in Volume 2. In the meantime, Democrats: keep pushing the envelope. Republicans: stop chasing old farts. Conservatives take your party back—leap and lead.

Remember, your vote counts!

About the Author

Raised in six foster homes but finding opportunity at every turn in America, after earning degrees, Professor George L. Fouke taught interdisciplinary studies and became chairman of the department of Politics at St. Andrews Presbyterian College in Laurinburg, North Carolina. He is the author of *Damn the Warocracy: A Plea to Restore American Democracy; The Global Architecture of Survival*: *Lessons from the Jewish Experience*; *Who Killed James the Just, the Brother of Jesus* (February 2015; historical novel about late Judaism/Early Christianity); and is completing *Twenty Christian and Jewish Samaritans.* He writes at the Tree House Bat Cave, North Carolina, and lives in Florida with his wife Dot near grand and great-grandchildren.